THE
Ethan Green
CHRONICLES

by
ERIC ORNER

St. Martin's Griffin
New York

To my cartoonist heroes:
Thomas Nast
Edward Gorey
David Levine
Roz Chast

Front and back cover designs by Judy Dombrowski

ISBN 0-312-14742-2

First St. Martin's Griffin Edition: February 1997

10 9 8 7 6 5 4 3 2 1

THE
Ethan Green
CHRONICLES

Also by Eric Orner

The Mostly Unfabulous Social Life of Ethan Green
Seven Deadly Sins of Love

Acknowledgments

Thank you to my mom, Rhoda Kaplan Pierce, to my brother, Peter Orner, and to my lover, Steve Parks, who deserves to be married to someone who'd give him big diamonds rather than lewd comic strips.

Thank you to my editor at St. Martin's Press, Keith Kahla, whose wisdom I depend on, and who, in allowing my three Ethan books to be published, has given me an experience for which I am terribly grateful.

Finally, a very special thanks to the indomitable Ardys Jane Kozbial, whose unenviable task it has been for the past six years to proofread and edit Ethan.

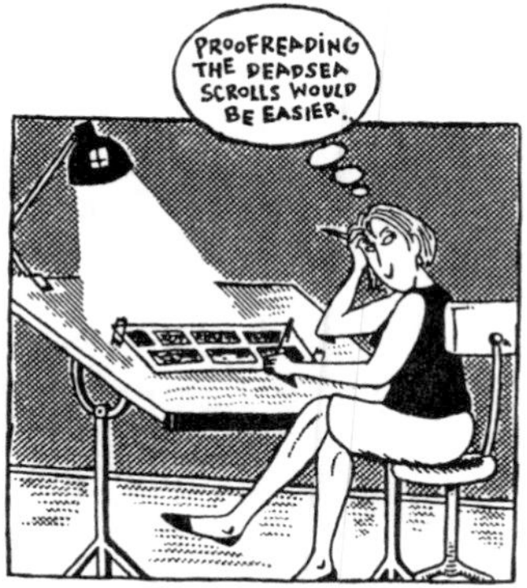
PROOFREADING THE DEADSEA SCROLLS WOULD BE EASIER.

Introduction

BY STEPHEN MCCAULEY

What exactly is it that makes Ethan Green's social life so determinedly and infamously unfabulous?

Is it his ex-lover Doug, the heartbreaker whose HIV status might or might not explain his inability to commit? Is it Etienne, his Montreal-based beau, a congenital liar who appears to be wanted by the Canadian Mounties? Maybe it's his shrink. From the looks of it, she's a chain-smoking psychic whose idea of therapeutic wisdom is to suggest Ethan chop up his ex-lover and make soup out of him. It's true, Ethan does spend a lot of time moping on his sofa and getting ready for social engagements he eventually opts out of. . . .

But unfabulous?

After all, the guy has close friends: the randy Hat Sisters, a pair of mustached drag queens who can be counted on to show up at the most inopportune moments; Charlotte, a buzz-cut lesbian never at a loss for a hardcore reality check or a solid piece of advice. He has a plump, perceptive cat. His mother is supportive. She goes to P-FLAG meetings and is on the lookout for a suitable man, preferably a podiatrist. Ethan even travels from time to time: P'town, Montreal, Des Moines. More often than not, he ends up letting his heart guide him instead of his head, but isn't that true for most of us?

Come to think of it, that might be it right there: What makes Ethan Green's social life unfabulous is that it's so familiar, so remarkably similar to our own. All those failed attempts at love, those hopeful, awkward evenings on the town. So many interminable parties followed by endless gossip sessions with friends.

And, ironically, it's that very quality of being instantly recognizable that makes *The Mostly Unfabulous Social Life of Ethan Green,* Eric Orner's comic strip, so determinedly, irresistibly, unflaggingly . . . well, fabulous.

Since 1990, Orner has been amusing us with Ethan and his loopy friends. Started as a weekly cartoon for Boston's *Bay Windows,* the strip is now syndicated in over sixty publications nationwide. In the past six years, nothing and everything has changed for Ethan. He doesn't appear to have aged much. He still hasn't settled into his life. He's no less socially awkward than he ever was. He hasn't got a steady boyfriend. He hasn't even moved.

On the other hand, Orner's strip has developed from a delightful comic confection, with lots of regional and inside jokes, into a seriously funny contribution to a new literary genre: the graphic short story. Like Lynda Barry, Roz Chast, Art Spiegleman, and even R. Crumb himself, Orner uses a potent combination of exactingly drawn cartoons and carefully chosen words to bring real people and the world they inhabit to vivid, three-dimensional life. Yes, there are still jokes, a few choice punch lines, some broadly sketched caricatures; but what stands out in this latest collection are the kinds of perfectly selected details you expect to find in solid literary fiction. Each character speaks in his own voice, gestures in his own style, behaves (or misbehaves) according to his own distinct psychology. And their stories, many of them connected, describe the angst, anxiety, and anguish of our times, even while they have us roaring with laughter. Without pretense or affectation, Eric Orner has given us a thoroughly appealing and accurate description of one corner of the gay experience in the waning days of this century. Few writers, working in any medium, have done it as well.

The Cast

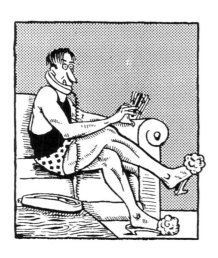

Ethan Green is the hero of these stories. He's looking for love and trying to avoid becoming insufferably jaded in the process.

Lucy is Ethan's cat. She could take him or leave him, but figures she'll stick around, at least until she figures out what's for dinner.

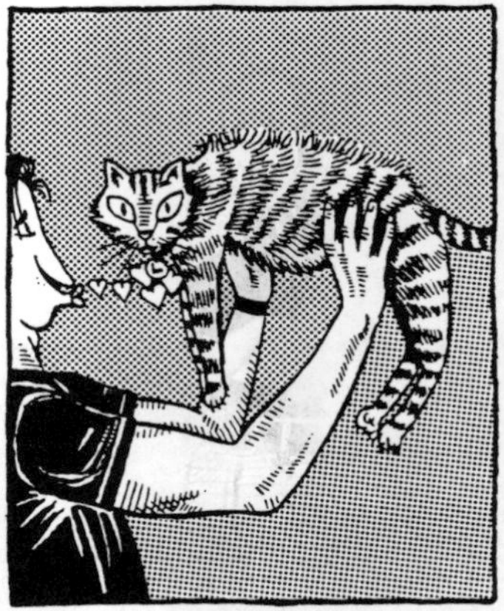

Bucky is Ethan's best friend. He's a big hearted, bartending, socially conscious circuit queen.

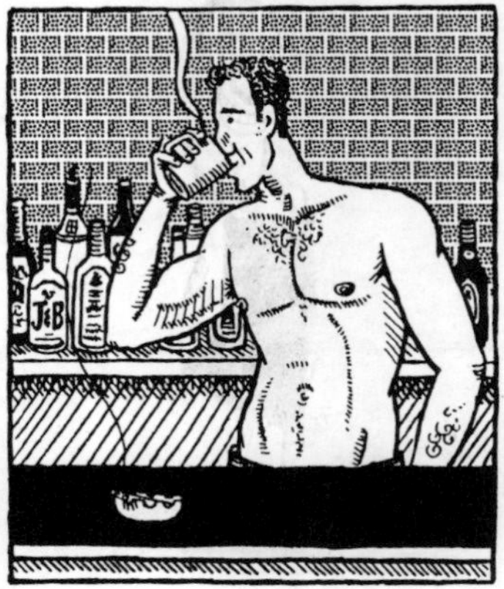
J&B

Charlotte is Ethan's neighbor. She's also his reality check, and the only person in his life who knows how to shoot a basket.

Todd is Ethan's arch nemesis anti-sister. He's a smarmy, noxious, social-climbing fink.

Doug is Ethan's "ex". He's the kind of guy who makes love to you atop the flannel shirt he removed, to spread over the sawdust he generated, building the bookshelves he's giving you for your birthday.

Etienne is Ethan's trick. He's wanted by the police.

ON THE OFF CHANCE THAT YOU ARE EXPERIENCING ONE OF THOSE TORRID SUMMER ROMANCES,

Perhaps you'll recognize

THE EIGHT FACES OF INFATUATION

WANTING
HEY.
HEY.
I'M JIM.
HEY.

NEEDING
Call me
487-LUVU

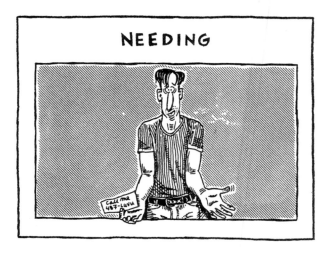

LUSTING

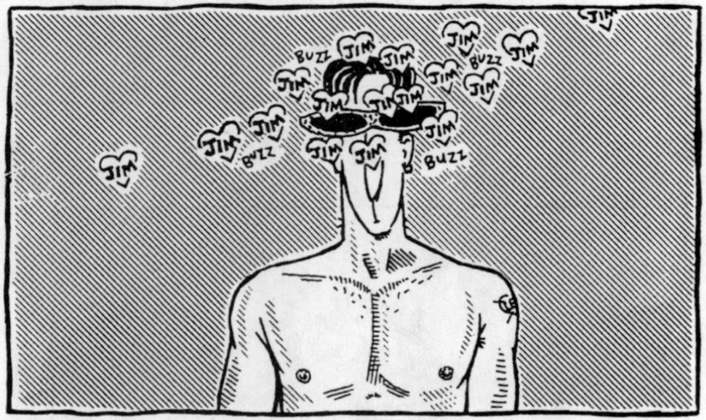
JIM
BUZZ
JIM
BUZZ
JIM
BUZZ
JIM
BUZZ

LONGING

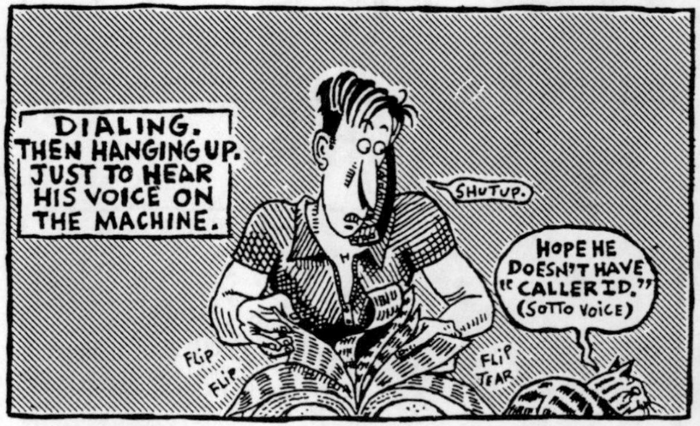
DIALING. THEN HANGING UP. JUST TO HEAR HIS VOICE ON THE MACHINE.
SHUTUP.
HOPE HE DOESN'T HAVE "CALLER ID." (SOTTO VOICE)
FLIP
FLIP
FLIP
TEAR

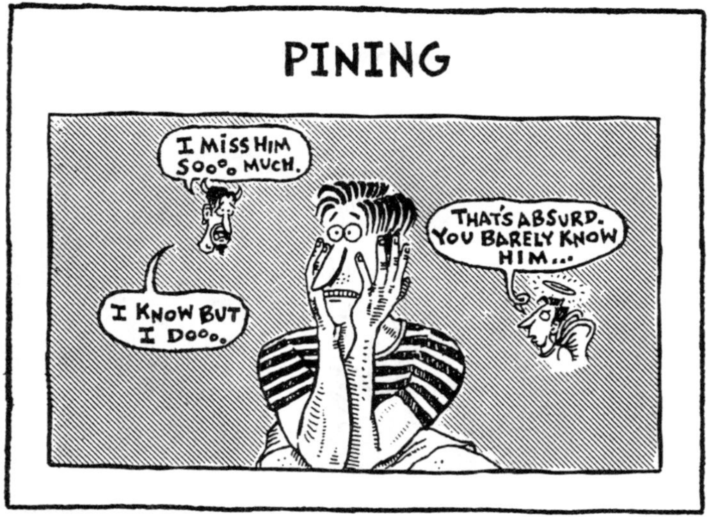
PINING
I MISS HIM SOOOO MUCH.
THAT'S ABSURD. YOU BARELY KNOW HIM...
I KNOW BUT I DOOOO.

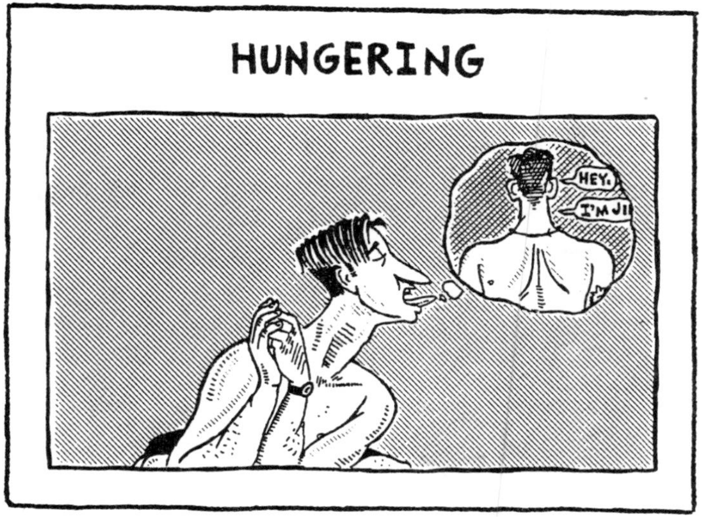
HUNGERING
HEY.
I'M JI

Continued...

CLINGING

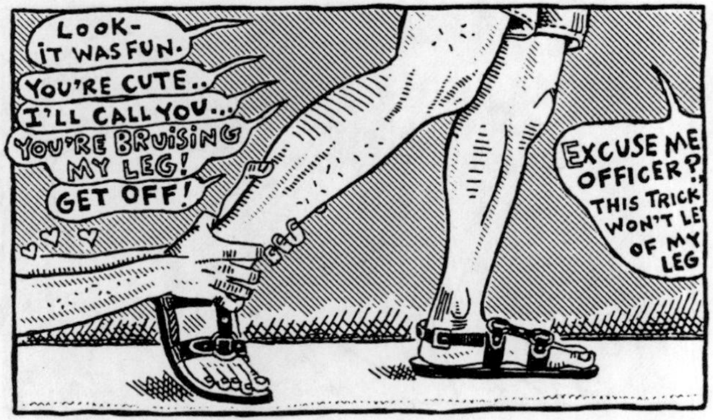
LOOK- IT WAS FUN.
YOU'RE CUTE..
I'LL CALL YOU...
YOU'RE BRUISING MY LEG!
GET OFF!
EXCUSE ME OFFICER? THIS TRICK WON'T LE OF MY LEG

DENYING

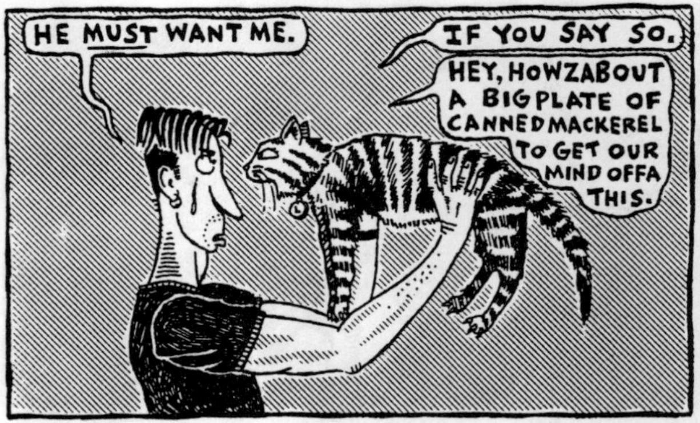
HE MUST WANT ME.
IF YOU SAY SO.
HEY, HOWZABOUT A BIG PLATE OF CANNED MACKEREL TO GET OUR MIND OFFA THIS.

end.

BEEFY SOPHOMORE LOVE SLAVES

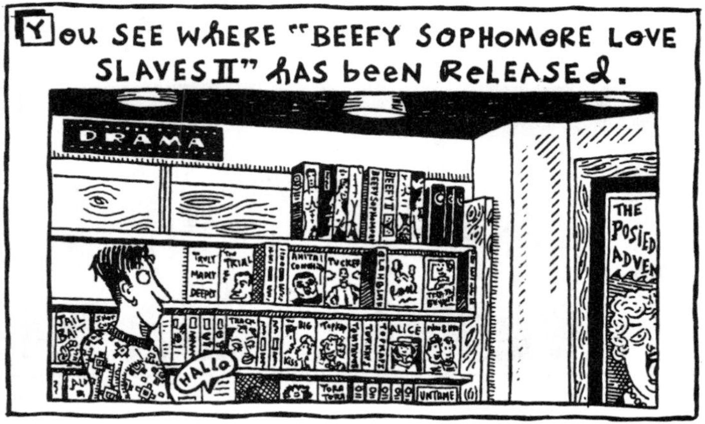
You see where "Beefy Sophomore Love Slaves II" has been released.
DRAMA
HALLO

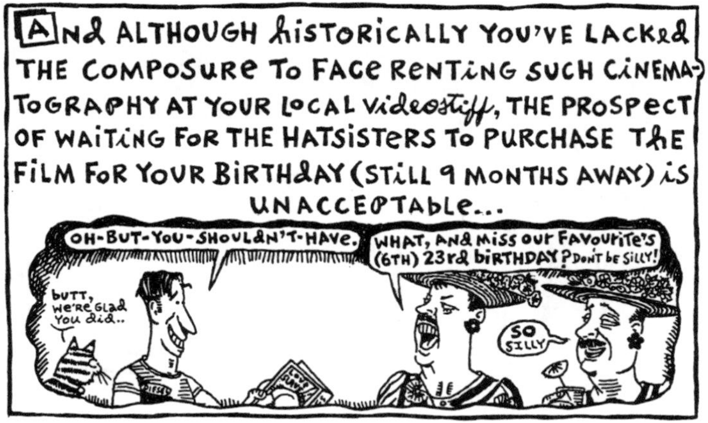
And although historically you've lacked the composure to face renting such cinema-tography at your local videostiff, the prospect of waiting for the Hatsisters to purchase the film for your birthday (still 9 months away) is unacceptable...
OH-BUT-YOU-SHOULDN'T-HAVE.
WHAT, AND MISS OUR FAVOURITE'S (6TH) 23rd BIRTHDAY? DON'T BE SILLY!
BUTT, WE'RE GLAD YOU DID..
SO SILLY

Continued...

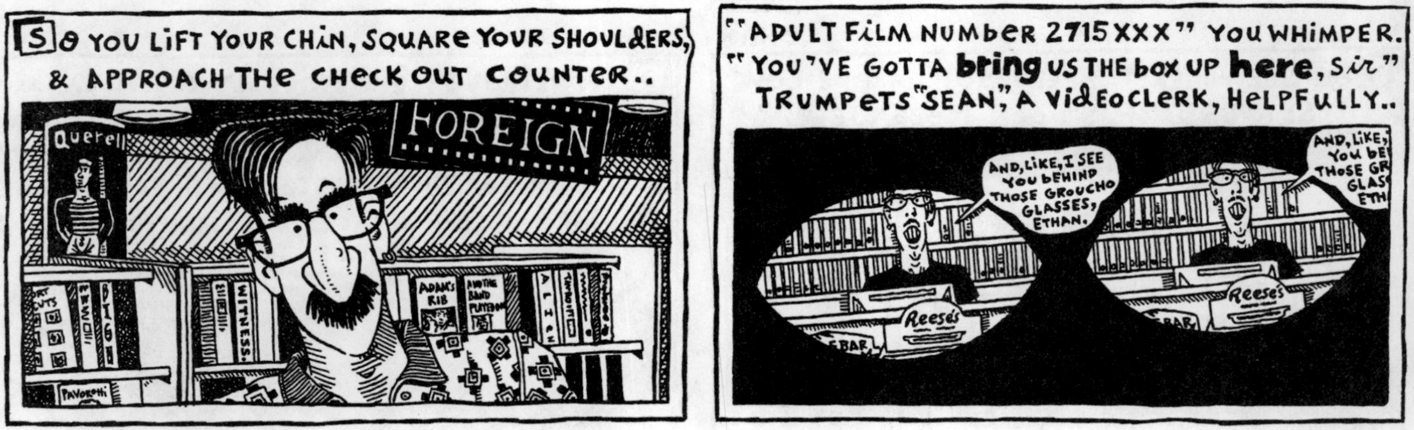
SO YOU LIFT YOUR CHIN, SQUARE YOUR SHOULDERS, & APPROACH THE CHECK OUT COUNTER..
FOREIGN
Querell
WITNESS.
ADAM'S RIB
ALIEN
PAVOROTTI
"ADULT FILM NUMBER 2715XXX" YOU WHIMPER.
"YOU'VE GOTTA **bring** US THE BOX UP **here**, *sir*"
TRUMPETS "SEAN," A VIDEOCLERK, HELPFULLY..
AND, LIKE, I SEE YOU BEHIND THOSE GROUCHO GLASSES, ETHAN.
Reese's
Reese's

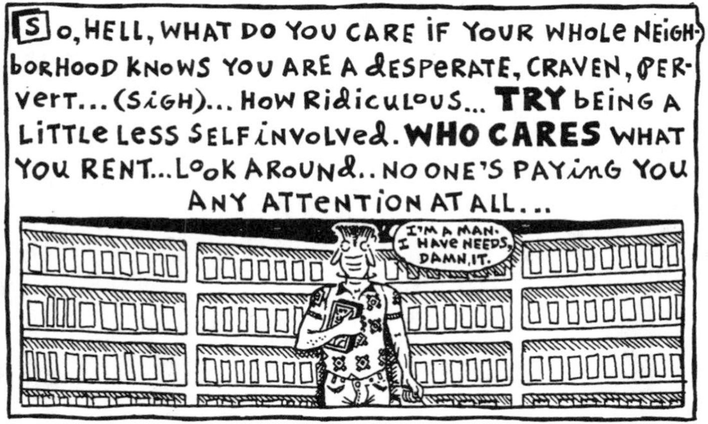
So, HELL, WHAT DO YOU CARE IF YOUR WHOLE NEIGH-BORHOOD KNOWS YOU ARE A DESPERATE, CRAVEN, PER-VERT... (SIGH)... HOW RIDICULOUS... **TRY** BEING A LITTLE LESS SELF INVOLVED. **WHO CARES** WHAT YOU RENT... LOOK AROUND.. NO ONE'S PAYING YOU ANY ATTENTION AT ALL...
I'M A MAN. I HAVE NEEDS, DAMN IT.

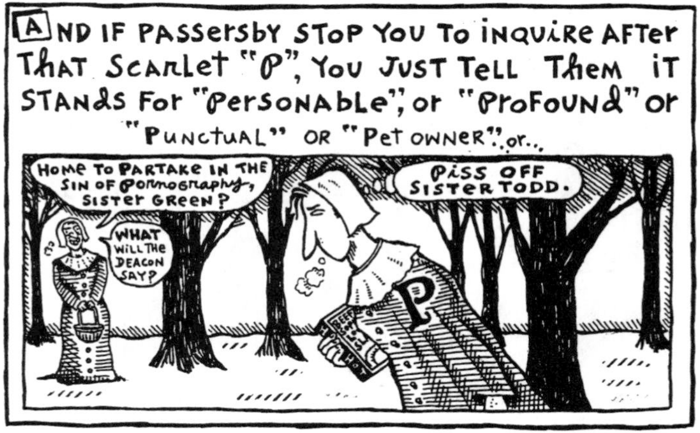
AND IF PASSERSBY STOP YOU TO INQUIRE AFTER THAT SCARLET "P", YOU JUST TELL THEM IT STANDS FOR "PERSONABLE", OR "PROFOUND" OR "PUNCTUAL" OR "PET OWNER"..OR..
HOME TO PARTAKE IN THE SIN OF PORNOGRAPHY, SISTER GREEN?
WHAT WILL THE DEACON SAY?
PISS OFF SISTER TODD.

end.

REGIONAL SURVEY:

SAUGATUCK MI.
HI, UH... I WAS WONDERING, DO YOU KNOW IF ANYONE IS HAVING A PARTY?
ACTUALLY, MY HOUSEMATES & I ARE! STOP BY! HEY THAT'd BE EXCELLENT. LEMME GIVE YA' DIRECTIONS.
PALM SPRINGS CA.
UH, HAVE YOU HEARD OF ANY PARTIES?
how Brassy!
YEA, I'VE HEARD OF A PARTY. YOU'RE LOOKING AT THE PARTY. THIS IS ALL THE PARTY YOU'RE GOING TO NEED, TO PARTY...

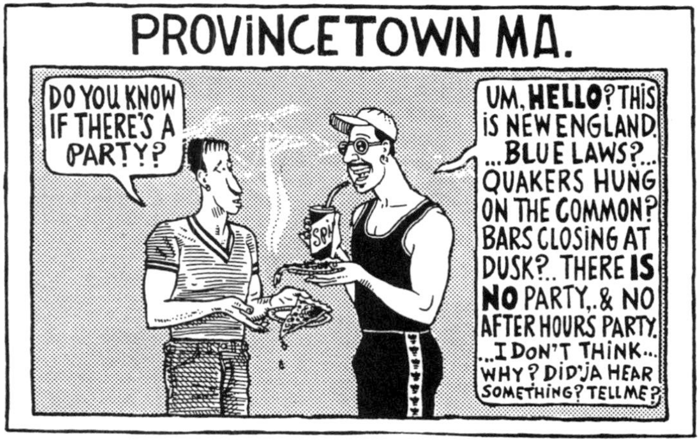
PROVINCETOWN MA.
DO YOU KNOW IF THERE'S A PARTY??
SPA
UM, HELLO? THIS IS NEW ENGLAND. ...BLUE LAWS?... QUAKERS HUNG ON THE COMMON? BARS CLOSING AT DUSK?.. THERE IS NO PARTY,. & NO AFTER HOURS PARTY. ...I DON'T THINK... WHY? DID'JA HEAR SOMETHING? TELL ME?

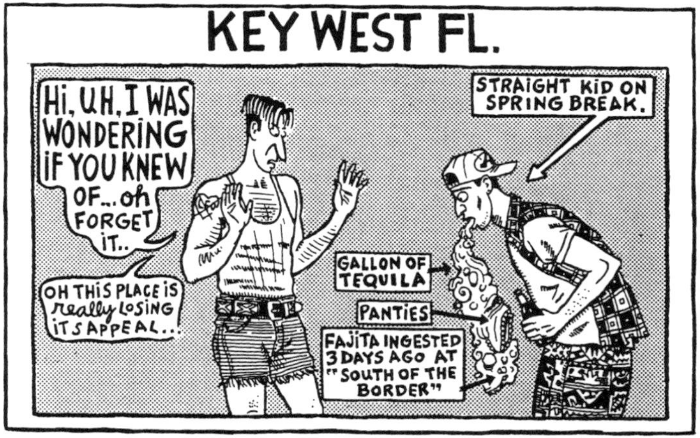
KEY WEST FL.
HI, UH, I WAS WONDERING IF YOU KNEW OF... oh FORGET IT..
OH THIS PLACE IS really LOSING ITS APPEAL...
STRAIGHT KID ON SPRING BREAK.
GALLON OF TEQUILA
PANTIES
FAJITA INGESTED 3 DAYS AGO AT "SOUTH OF THE BORDER"

Continued...

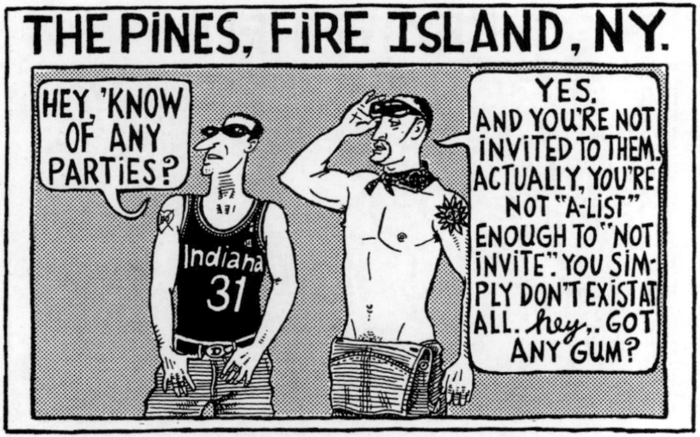
THE PINES, FIRE ISLAND, NY.
HEY, 'KNOW OF ANY PARTIES?
Indiana 31
YES. AND YOU'RE NOT INVITED TO THEM. ACTUALLY, YOU'RE NOT "A-LIST" ENOUGH TO "NOT INVITE". YOU SIMPLY DON'T EXIST AT ALL. hey,. GOT ANY GUM?

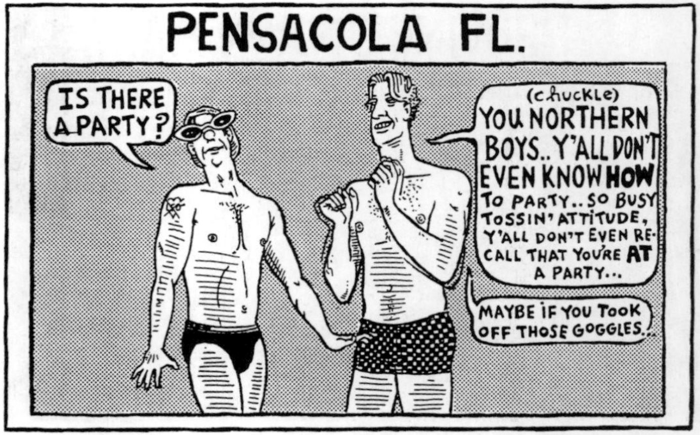
PENSACOLA FL.
IS THERE A PARTY?
(chuckle) YOU NORTHERN BOYS.. Y'ALL DON'T EVEN KNOW HOW TO PARTY.. SO BUSY TOSSIN' ATTITUDE, Y'ALL DON'T EVEN RECALL THAT YOU'RE AT A PARTY...
MAYBE IF YOU TOOK OFF THOSE GOGGLES..

end.

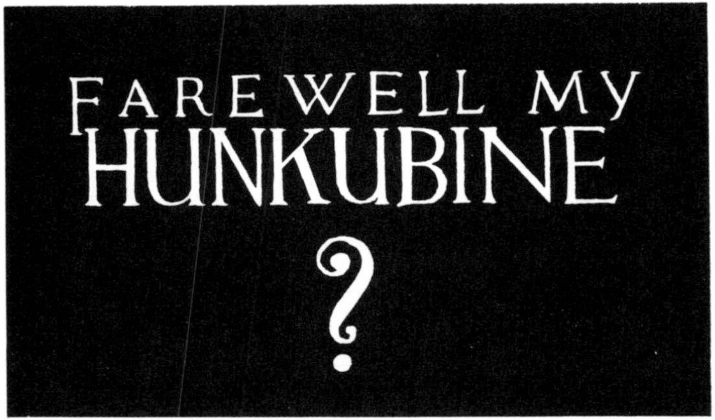
FAREWELL MY
HUNKUBINE
?

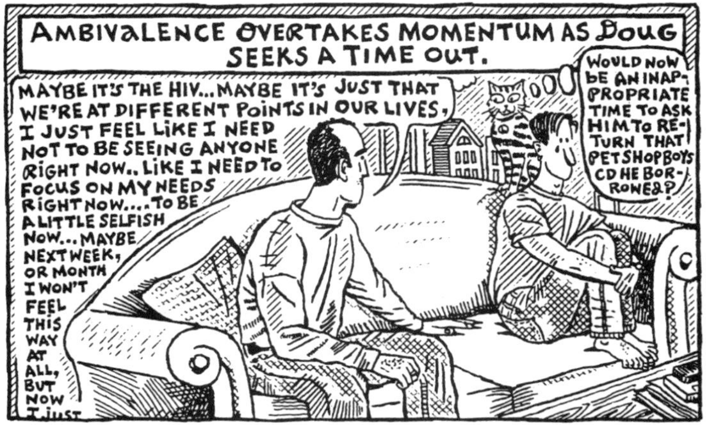
AMBIVALENCE OVERTAKES MOMENTUM AS DOUG SEEKS A TIME OUT.
MAYBE IT'S THE HIV...MAYBE IT'S JUST THAT WE'RE AT DIFFERENT POINTS IN OUR LIVES, I JUST FEEL LIKE I NEED NOT TO BE SEEING ANYONE RIGHT NOW.. LIKE I NEED TO FOCUS ON MY NEEDS RIGHT NOW.... TO BE A LITTLE SELFISH NOW... MAYBE NEXT WEEK, OR MONTH I WON'T FEEL THIS WAY AT ALL, BUT NOW I JUST
WOULD NOW BE AN INAP-PROPRIATE TIME TO ASK HIM TO RE-TURN THAT PET SHOP BOYS CD HE BOR-ROWED?

Continued...

BEEPBEEPBEEPBEEPBEEP.
(PAUSE)
BEEPBEEPBEEPBEEPBEEP.
(CLICK)
HI... THIS IS ETHAN, I'M NOT IN NOW, LEAVE ME A MESSAGE & I'LL CALL BACK.
(TONE)
EETH, IT'S DOUG, PICK UP. ETHAN?.. WELL.. OK,. I, UH, JUST WANTED TO MAKE SURE YOU'RE OK?.. EETH? WELL.. OK.. I'LL CALL LATER..

MAN TROUBLE:
PLEASE STAND BY.

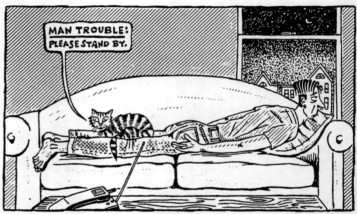

I'M GOING TO HOPE THAT YOU AREN'T SO SELFISH AS TO BE JUST SITTING AROUND OUT THERE WAITING TO BE ENTERTAINED THIS WEEK, AFTER WHAT I'VE JUST BEEN PUT THROUGH?! ...TALK ABOUT INSENSITIVE...
SHEESH...
I MEAN, YOU WANT LAUGHS, GO READ "FAMILY CIRCUS".
HE'S BEEN LIKE THIS FOR DAYS..
GOSH CHARLOTTE, HOW WILL WE EVER BREAK HIM OUT OF THIS STUPOR?
WE'LL START BY TELLING HIM *Cincinnati* JUST ACCIDENTALLY ELECTED A DYKE MAYOR..
IT DID?
LE

end.

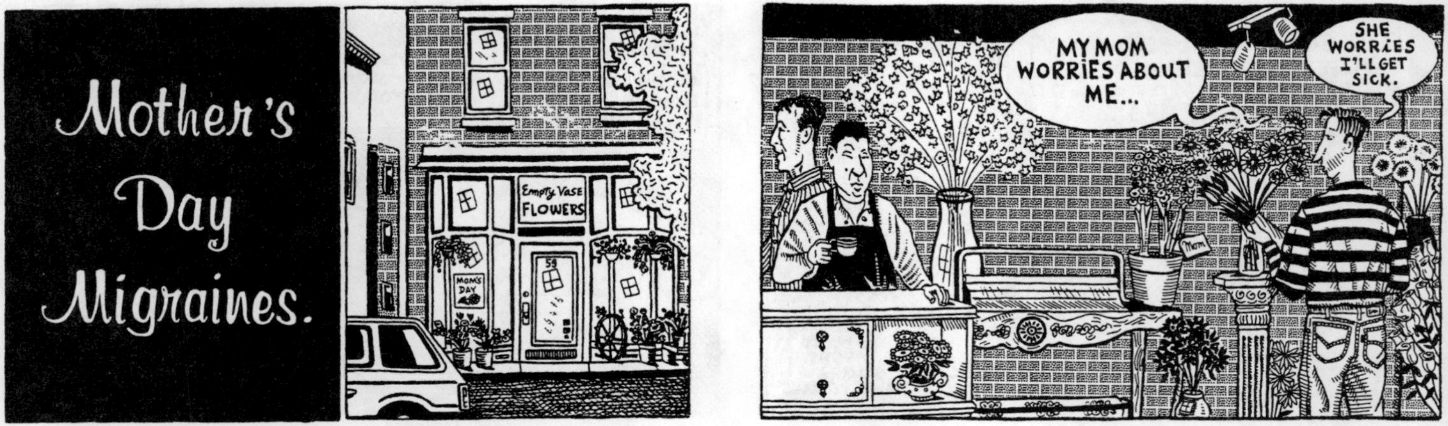
Mother's Day Migraines.
Empty Vase FLOWERS
59
MOM'S DAY
MY MOM WORRIES ABOUT ME...
Mom
SHE WORRIES I'LL GET SICK.

SHE WORRIES MY BEING GAY MEANS PEOPLE WILL TREAT ME BADLY.
SHE WORRIES I WON'T BE *happy*...
SHE WORRIES MY CAREER WILL SUFFER...
CAREER? I DIDN'T EVEN KNOW HE HAD A JOB...

Continued...

SHE WORRIES YOU'LL BORROW AND STRETCH OUT HER GOOD PUMPS...
WORRYING ABOUT ME. IT'S MY MOTHER'S FULL TIME JOB.
TOO BAD THERE'S NOT MORE OF YOU, WE'D HAVE FULL MOM EMPLOYMENT.
END

FIELD GUIDE PART 1...

OKAY, SO YOU'RE ON A BUSINESS OR PLEASURE OR FAMILY-RELATED TRIP TO AN UNFAMILIAR CITY. WELL SWEETIE, TRAVELING IS HASSLE ENUF, THANKS VERY MUCH, WITHOUT HAVING TO STAND AROUND LIKE YOU'RE FRESH OFF THE TURNIP TRUCK, TRYING TO DIVINE WHICH BELLHOP, WAITER, OR GUY IN THE HOTEL GYM'S A BIG QUEEN. THIS BEING THE CASE,

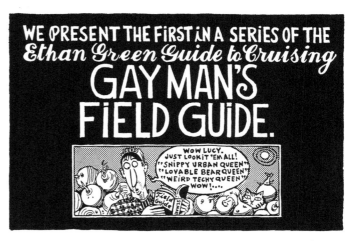

WE PRESENT THE FIRST IN A SERIES OF THE *Ethan Green Guide to Cruising*

GAY MAN'S FIELD GUIDE.

WOW LUCY, JUST LOOKIT 'EM ALL! "SNIPPY URBAN QUEEN" "LOVABLE BEAR QUEEN" "WEIRD TECHY QUEEN" WOW!...

Continued...

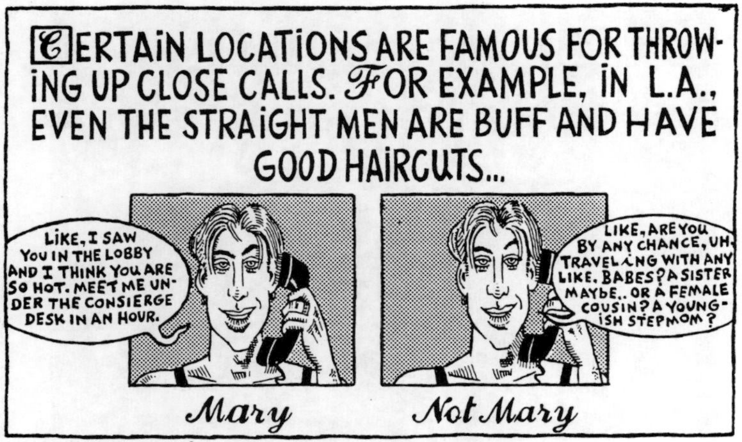
CERTAIN LOCATIONS ARE FAMOUS FOR THROWING UP CLOSE CALLS. FOR EXAMPLE, IN L.A., EVEN THE STRAIGHT MEN ARE BUFF AND HAVE GOOD HAIRCUTS...
LIKE, I SAW YOU IN THE LOBBY AND I THINK YOU ARE SO HOT. MEET ME UNDER THE CONSIERGE DESK IN AN HOUR.
LIKE, ARE YOU BY ANY CHANCE, UH, TRAVELING WITH ANY LIKE. BABES? A SISTER MAYBE.. OR A FEMALE COUSIN? A YOUNG-ISH STEPMOM?
Mary
Not Mary

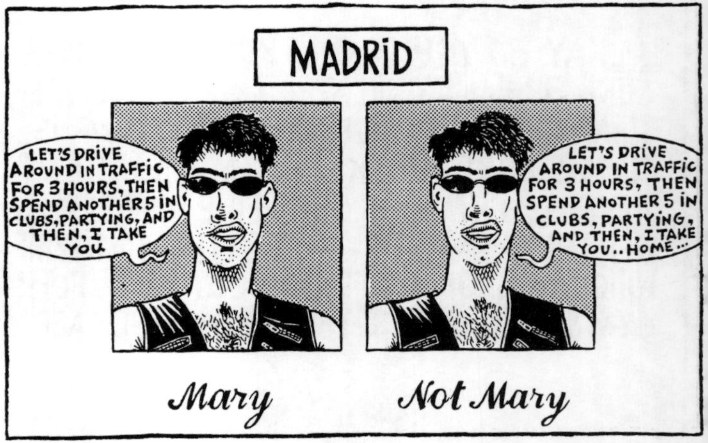
MADRID
LET'S DRIVE AROUND IN TRAFFIC FOR 3 HOURS, THEN SPEND ANOTHER 5 IN CLUBS, PARTYING, AND THEN, I TAKE YOU
LET'S DRIVE AROUND IN TRAFFIC FOR 3 HOURS, THEN SPEND ANOTHER 5 IN CLUBS, PARTYING, AND THEN, I TAKE YOU.. HOME...
Mary
Not Mary

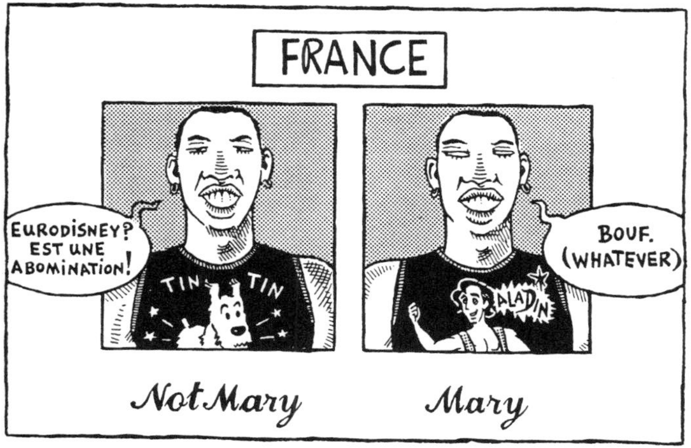
FRANCE
EURODISNEY? EST UNE ABOMINATION!
TIN TIN
ALADIN
BOUF. (WHATEVER)
Not Mary
Mary

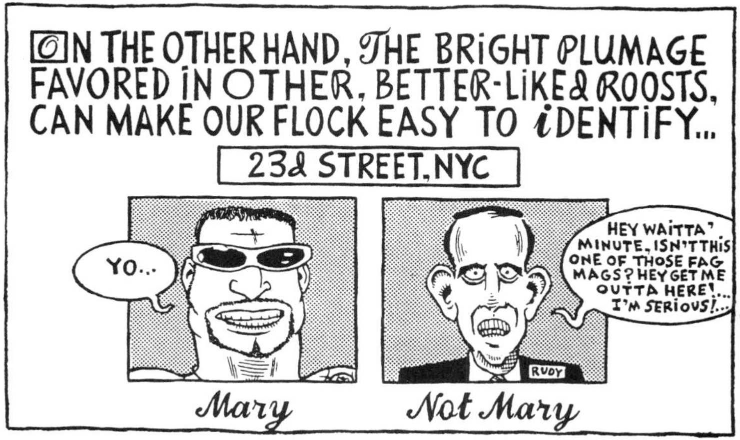
ON THE OTHER HAND, THE BRIGHT PLUMAGE FAVORED IN OTHER, BETTER-LIKED ROOSTS, CAN MAKE OUR FLOCK EASY TO IDENTIFY...
23d STREET, NYC
YO...
HEY WAITTA' MINUTE, ISN'T THIS ONE OF THOSE FAG MAGS? HEY GET ME OUTTA HERE!... I'M SERIOUS!...
RUDY
Mary
Not Mary

END.

THE ETHAN GREEN "IT'S NOT
IT'S WHY YOU STAYED TOGETHER

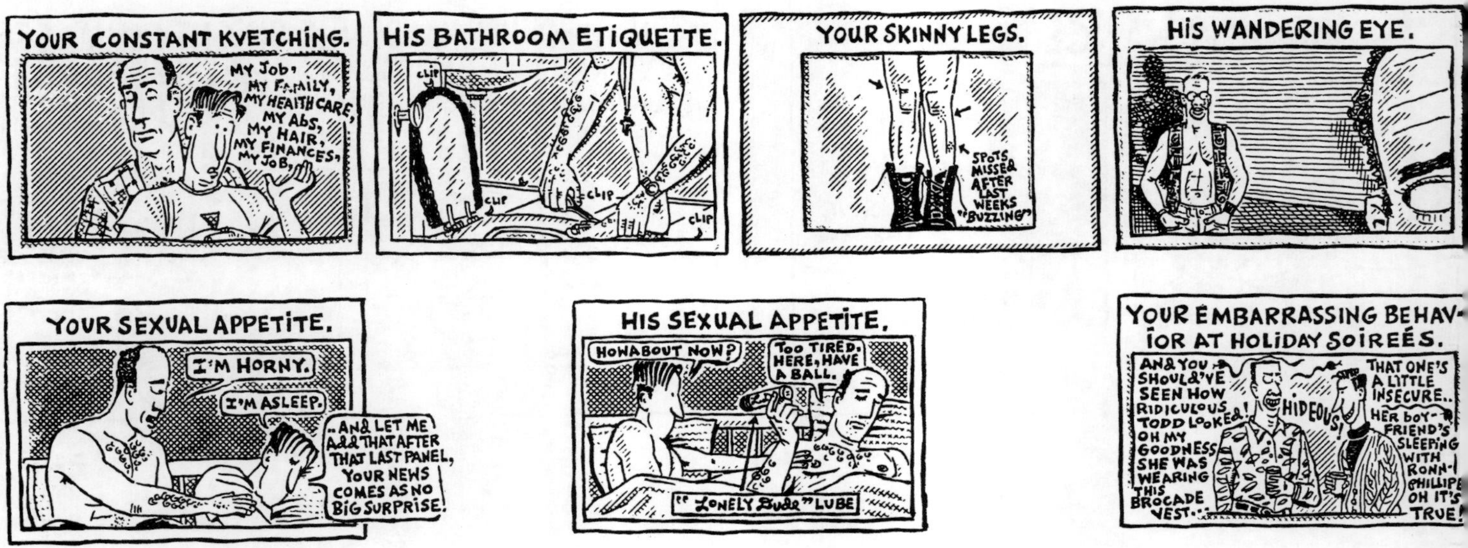

YOUR CONSTANT KVETCHING.
MY JOB, MY FAMILY, MY HEALTH CARE, MY ABS, MY HAIR, MY FINANCES, MY JOB,
HIS BATHROOM ETIQUETTE.
CLIP
CLIP
CLIP
CLIP
YOUR SKINNY LEGS.
SPOTS MISSED AFTER LAST WEEKS "BUZZING"
HIS WANDERING EYE.
YOUR SEXUAL APPETITE.
I'M HORNY.
I'M ASLEEP.
..AND LET ME ADD THAT AFTER THAT LAST PANEL, YOUR NEWS COMES AS NO BIG SURPRISE.
HIS SEXUAL APPETITE.
HOW ABOUT NOW?
TOO TIRED. HERE, HAVE A BALL.
"LONELY DUDE" LUBE
YOUR EMBARRASSING BEHAVIOR AT HOLIDAY SOIREÉS.
AND YOU SHOULD'VE SEEN HOW RIDICULOUS TODD LOOKED! OH MY GOODNESS SHE WAS WEARING THIS BROCADE VEST...
HIDEOUS!
THAT ONE'S A LITTLE INSECURE.. HER BOY-FRIEND'S SLEEPING WITH RONN-PHILLIPE OH IT'S TRUE!

WHY THE TWO OF YOU BROKE UP, AS LONG AS YOU DID." SURVEY:

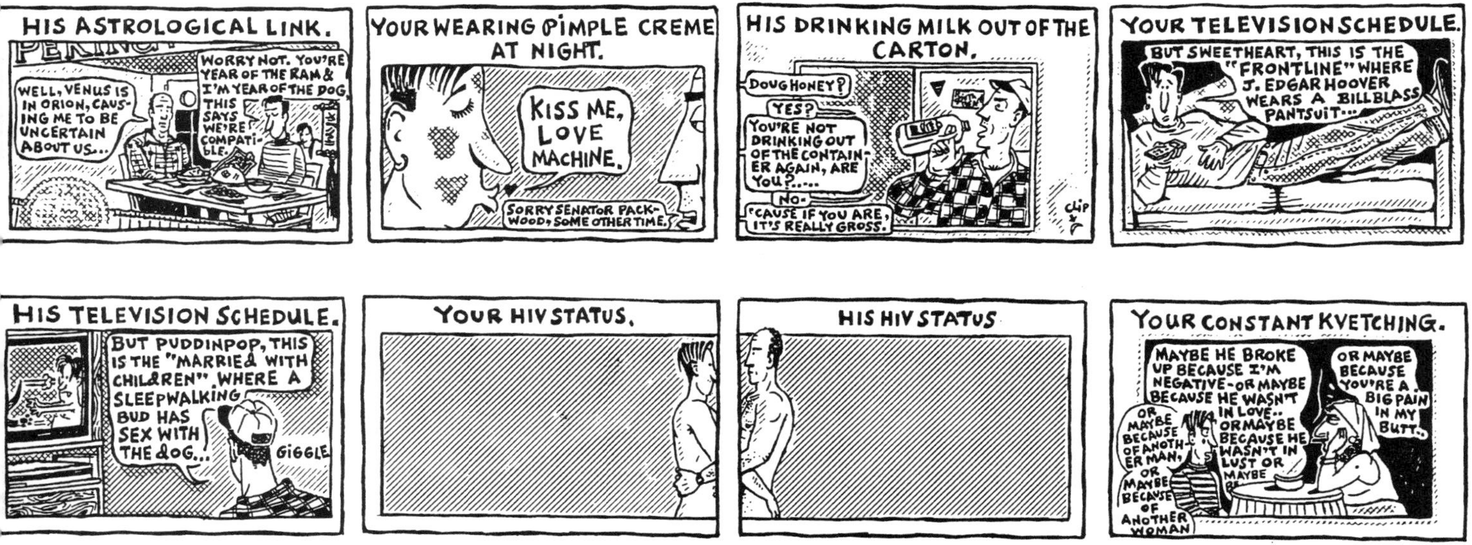
HIS ASTROLOGICAL LINK.
WELL, VENUS IS IN ORION, CAUSING ME TO BE UNCERTAIN ABOUT US...
WORRY NOT. YOU'RE YEAR OF THE RAM & I'M YEAR OF THE DOG. THIS SAYS WE'RE COMPATIBLE.
YOUR WEARING PIMPLE CREME AT NIGHT.
KISS ME, LOVE MACHINE.
SORRY SENATOR PACKWOOD, SOME OTHER TIME.
HIS DRINKING MILK OUT OF THE CARTON.
DOUG HONEY?
YES?
YOU'RE NOT DRINKING OUT OF THE CONTAINER AGAIN, ARE YOU?....
NO-
'CAUSE IF YOU ARE, IT'S REALLY GROSS.
YOUR TELEVISION SCHEDULE.
BUT SWEETHEART, THIS IS THE "FRONTLINE" WHERE J. EDGAR HOOVER WEARS A BILL BLASS PANTSUIT...
HIS TELEVISION SCHEDULE.
BUT PUDDINPOP, THIS IS THE "MARRIED WITH CHILDREN", WHERE A SLEEPWALKING BUD HAS SEX WITH THE DOG...
GIGGLE
YOUR HIV STATUS.
HIS HIV STATUS
YOUR CONSTANT KVETCHING.
MAYBE HE BROKE UP BECAUSE I'M NEGATIVE-OR MAYBE BECAUSE HE WASN'T IN LOVE.. OR MAYBE BECAUSE HE WASN'T IN LUST OR MAYBE
OR MAYBE BECAUSE OF ANOTHER MAN, OR MAYBE BECAUSE OF ANOTHER WOMAN
OR MAYBE BECAUSE YOU'RE A BIG PAIN IN MY BUTT..

end.

SLIDE SHOW.

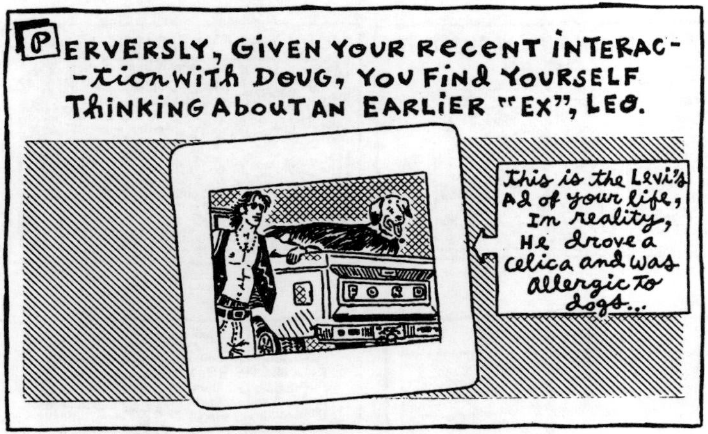
PERVERSLY, GIVEN YOUR RECENT INTERAC-TION WITH DOUG, YOU FIND YOURSELF THINKING ABOUT AN EARLIER "EX", LEO.
FORD
This is the Levi's Ad of your life, In reality, He drove a celica and was allergic to dogs...

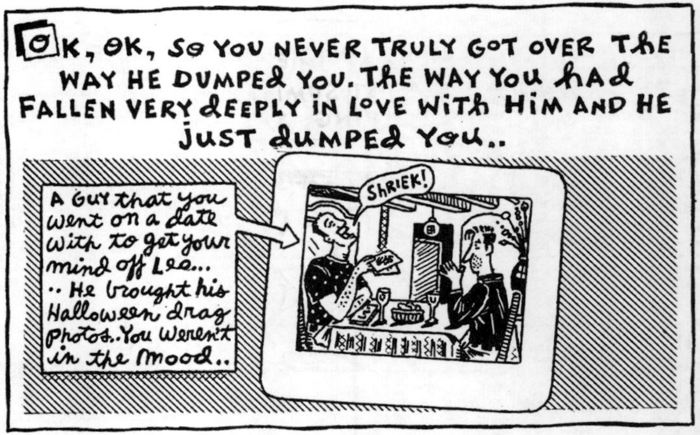
OK, OK, SO YOU NEVER TRULY GOT OVER THE WAY HE DUMPED YOU. THE WAY YOU HAD FALLEN VERY DEEPLY IN LOVE WITH HIM AND HE JUST DUMPED YOU..
A GUY that you went on a date with to get your mind off Leo... .. He brought his Halloween drag photos.. You weren't in the mood..
SHRIEK!

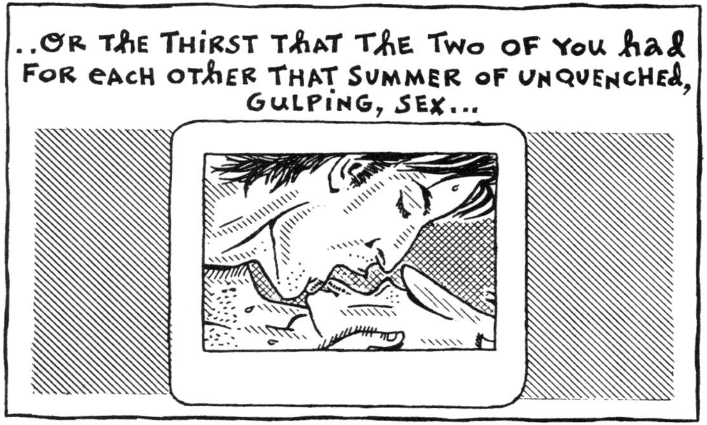
..OR THE THIRST THAT THE TWO OF YOU HAD FOR EACH OTHER THAT SUMMER OF UNQUENCHED, GULPING, SEX...

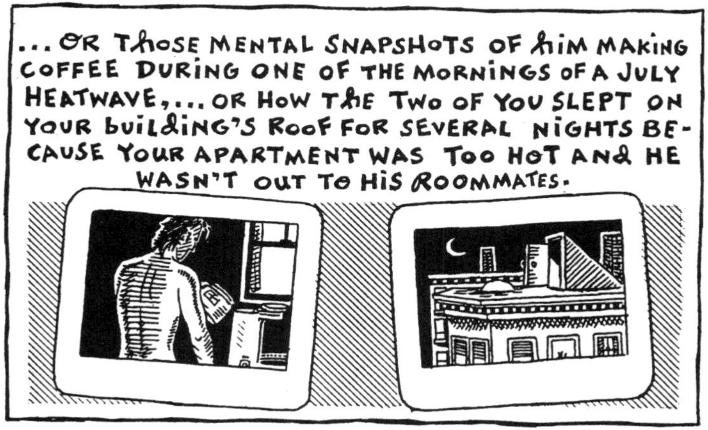
...OR THOSE MENTAL SNAPSHOTS OF HIM MAKING COFFEE DURING ONE OF THE MORNINGS OF A JULY HEATWAVE,... OR HOW THE TWO OF YOU SLEPT ON YOUR BUILDING'S ROOF FOR SEVERAL NIGHTS BE-CAUSE YOUR APARTMENT WAS TOO HOT AND HE WASN'T OUT TO HIS ROOMMATES.

Continued...

...BUT WAIT, IF YOU'RE DEPRESSED ABOUT DOUG, WHY IN HELL IS YOUR BRAIN GIVING THIS SLIDE SHOW OF LEO?
Affection For Agnes Moorehead Lobe.

YOUR THERAPIST, ZOLNA, SAYS YOU NEED TO WORK ON LETTING GO.
"Ex" lovers should be chopped up, mixed with garden vegetables, and added to a nice Broth.
WAIT- YOU'RE SAYING TURN THEM INTO SOUP?
RIGHT.
OH...

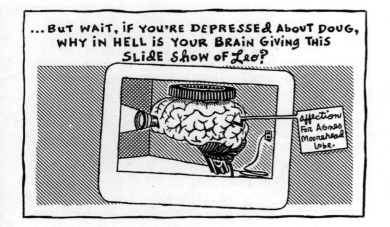

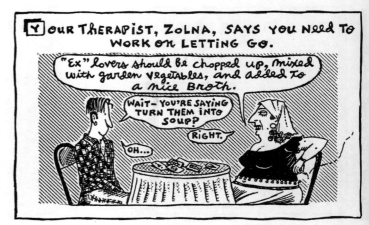

end.

how we dance
(Part 1)
With Ethan Green
MISS GLACIAL
NICE TO WATCH... ABOUT AS MUCH FUN AS AN EARLY MORNING ROOT CANAL.
WOW YOU ARE SO BEAUTIFUL
HOW'BOUT A KISS?
LIL' BUSS ON THE CHEEK?
HANDSHAKE? EXCHANGE OF POSTCARDS?
"PLEASE" NO TOUCHING
NO.
NOPE.
UHUH.
THE MAMBO KING
DANCES TO EVERYTHING AS HE IMAGINES DESI ARNAZ MIGHT'VE.
QUAN, THE DJ IS PLAYING TAPESTRY BY CAROL KING. I'M NOT SURE THAT DANCING THE LIMBO IS APPROPRIATE

Continued...

THE BEAT CATCHER

SEEMS TO BE PREOCCUPIED WITH PICKING IMAGINARY LIGHTNING BUGS OUT OF THIN AIR.

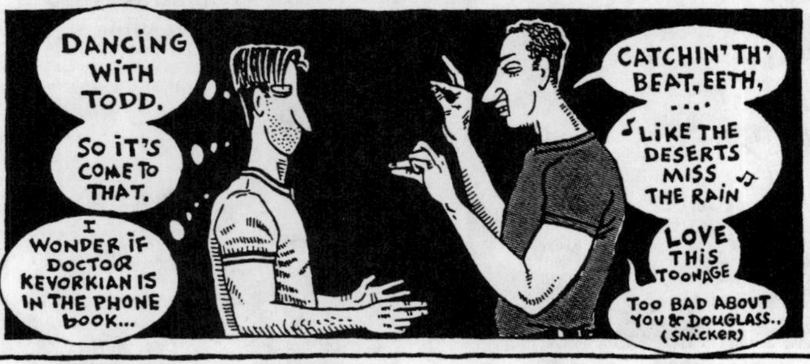
DANCING WITH TODD.
SO IT'S COME TO THAT.
I WONDER IF DOCTOR KEVORKIAN IS IN THE PHONE BOOK...
CATCHIN' TH' BEAT, EETH, ...
♪ LIKE THE DESERTS MISS THE RAIN ♫
LOVE THIS TOONAGE
TOO BAD ABOUT YOU & DOUGLASS.. (SNICKER)

THE BABBLER

NEEDS TO TALK TO YOU **RIGHT NOW**, HERE ON THE FLOOR, ABOUT HIS CAREER, FAMILY PROBLEMS, THE FACT THAT HE IS SLEEPING WITH SOMEONE YOU WANT TO SLEEP WITH, PROSPECTS FOR EUROPEAN MONETARY UNION, BODY ISSUES, WHO HE HATES, ETC, ETC...

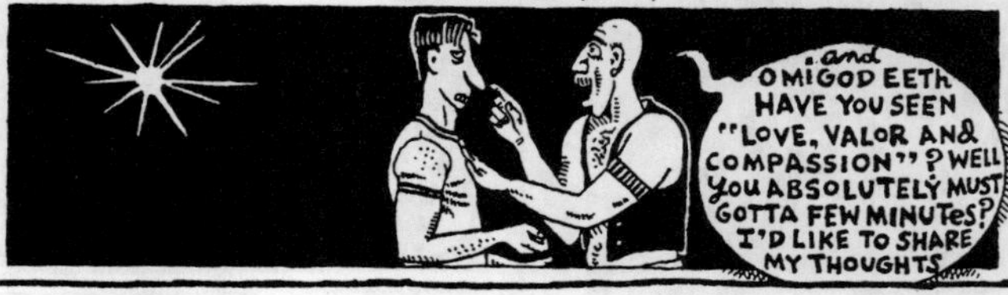
..and OMIGOD EETH HAVE YOU SEEN "LOVE, VALOR AND COMPASSION"? WELL YOU ABSOLUTELY MUST GOTTA FEW MINUTES? I'D LIKE TO SHARE MY THOUGHTS

THE SLANKERS

COME CLOSEST TO ACTUALLY HAVING SEX RIGHT ON THE FLOOR. IRONIC, BECAUSE WHAT PUTS THEM ON THE ROAD OFTEN PREVENTS THEM FROM REACHING THE DESTINATION...

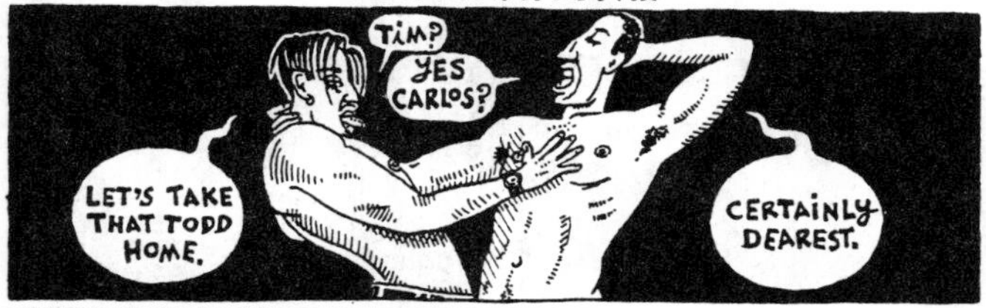
TIM?
YES CARLOS?
LET'S TAKE THAT TODD HOME.
CERTAINLY DEAREST.

THE DJ GROUPIE

CLOSE COUSIN OF THE BABBLER. FEELS COMPELLED TO POINT OUT TO YOU THE NUANCES OF EACH SONG.

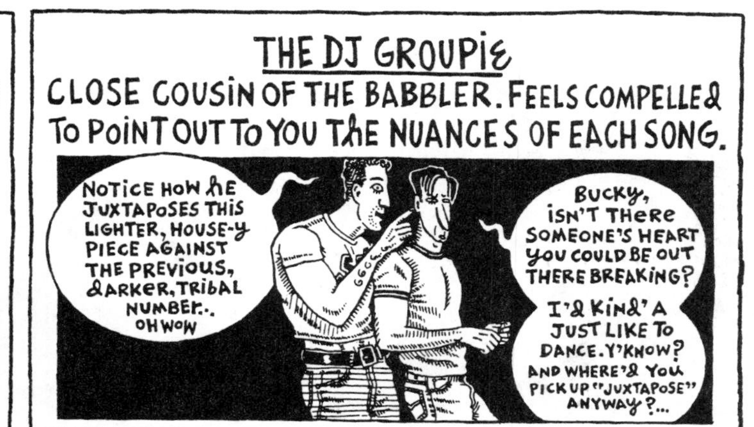
NOTICE HOW HE JUXTAPOSES THIS LIGHTER, HOUSE-Y PIECE AGAINST THE PREVIOUS, DARKER, TRIBAL NUMBER.. OH WOW
BUCKY, ISN'T THERE SOMEONE'S HEART YOU COULD BE OUT THERE BREAKING?
I'D KIND'A JUST LIKE TO DANCE. Y'KNOW?
AND WHERE'D YOU PICK UP "JUXTAPOSE" ANYWAY?...

end.

how we dance
(Part 2)
With Ethan Green

THE POINTER
HELPFULLY IDENTIFIES YOU, THEN THE CEILING, THEN YOU, THEN THE CEILING, THEN YOU AGAIN, THEN THE CEILING AGAIN, Well, You Get The Picture..

BUCKY, I'M ABOUT 3 SECONDS from SNAPPING THOSE FINGERS OFF, FYI.

HUSH ETHAN, I'M PEAKING.

PECS
WITHIN 5 MINUTES OF HIM REMOVING HIS SHIRT, EVERYONE HAS REMOVED THEIR SHIRTS..

DOUG

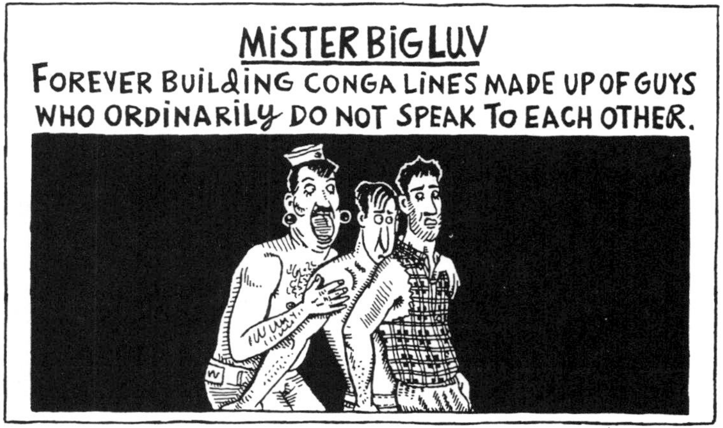
MISTER BIGLUV
FOREVER BUILDING CONGA LINES MADE UP OF GUYS WHO ORDINARILY DO NOT SPEAK TO EACH OTHER.

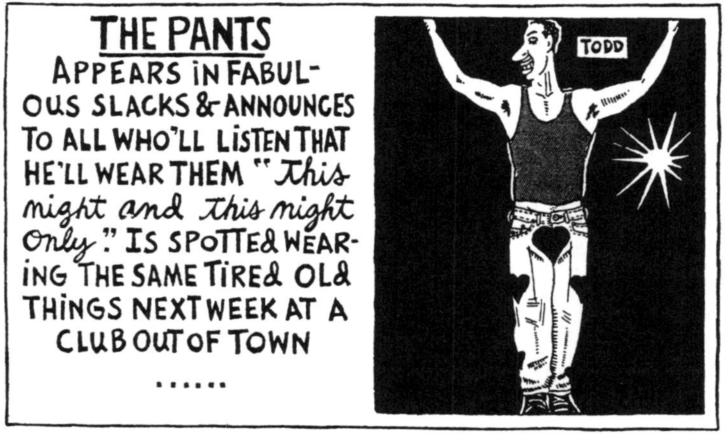
THE PANTS
APPEARS IN FABULOUS SLACKS & ANNOUNCES TO ALL WHO'LL LISTEN THAT HE'LL WEAR THEM "this night and this night Only." IS SPOTTED WEARING THE SAME TIRED OLD THINGS NEXT WEEK AT A CLUB OUT OF TOWN
......
TODD

Continued...

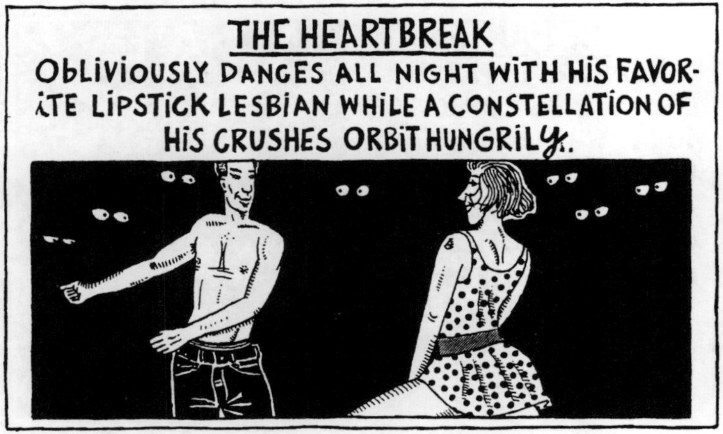
THE HEARTBREAK
OBLIVIOUSLY DANCES ALL NIGHT WITH HIS FAVORITE LIPSTICK LESBIAN WHILE A CONSTELLATION OF HIS CRUSHES ORBIT HUNGRILY..

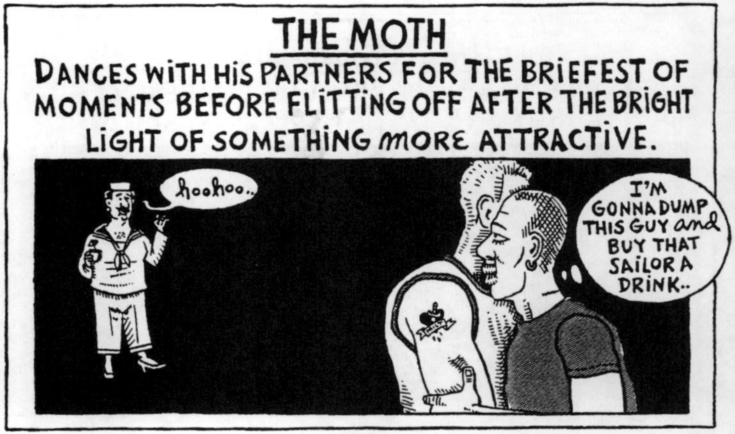
THE MOTH
DANCES WITH HIS PARTNERS FOR THE BRIEFEST OF MOMENTS BEFORE FLITTING OFF AFTER THE BRIGHT LIGHT OF SOMETHING MORE ATTRACTIVE.
hoohoo..
I'M GONNA DUMP THIS GUY and BUY THAT SAILOR A DRINK..

end.

TODD'S PARTY

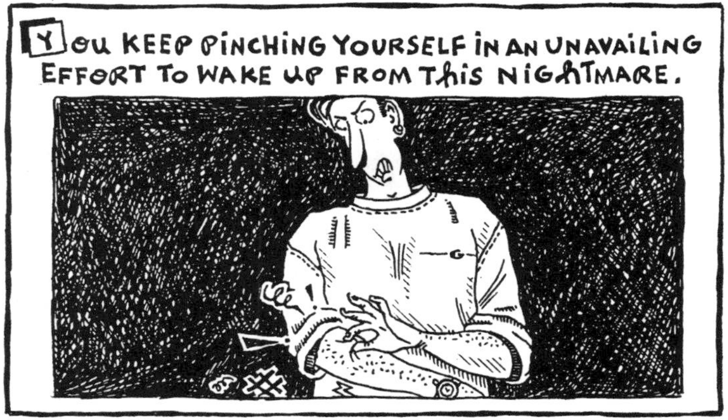
YOU KEEP PINCHING YOURSELF IN AN UNAVAILING EFFORT TO WAKE UP FROM THIS NIGHTMARE.

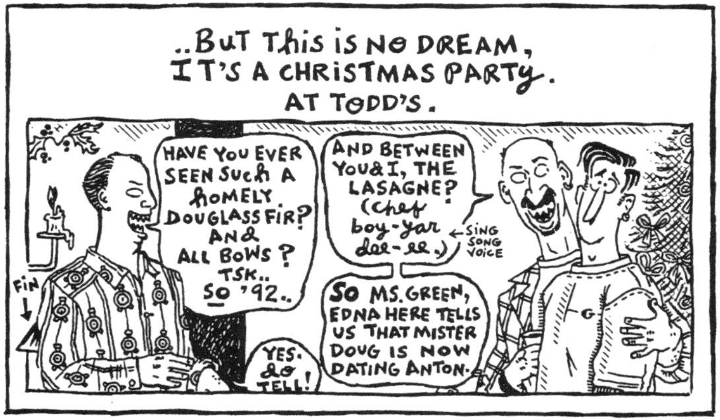
..BUT THIS IS NO DREAM, IT'S A CHRISTMAS PARTY. AT TODD'S.
HAVE YOU EVER SEEN SUCH A HOMELY DOUGLASS FIR? AND ALL BOWS? TSK.. SO '92..
AND BETWEEN YOU & I, THE LASAGNE? (Chef boy-yar dee-ee.)
← SING SONG VOICE
SO MS. GREEN, EDNA HERE TELLS US THAT MISTER DOUG IS NOW DATING ANTON.
YES. do TELL!
FIN ↓

Continued...

YOU WARILY EYEBALL THE OTHER ATTENDEES.
COMPETITION FOR BEST *holiday* blouse is SiLENT,
but FiERCE.

POOR, STUPiD TODD iS WEARiNG *last year's*
INTERNATIONAL MALE® "SWASHBUCKLER" SHiRT
HE WiLL BE RidiCULEd WELL iNTO FEBRUARY...

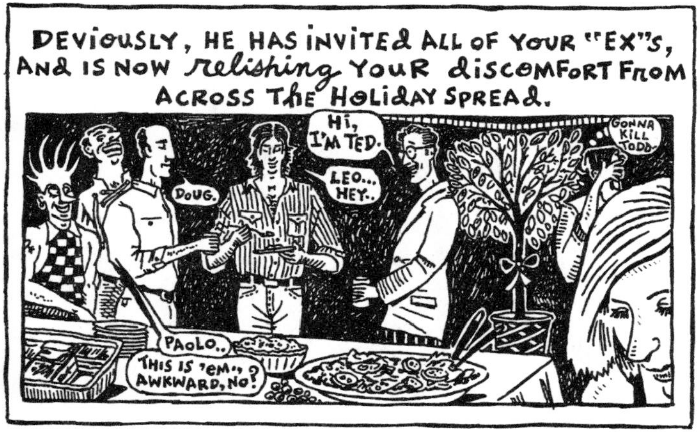
DEVIOUSLY, HE HAS INVITED ALL OF YOUR "EX"'S, AND IS NOW *relishing* YOUR DISCOMFORT FROM ACROSS THE HOLIDAY SPREAD.
DOUG.
HI, I'M TED.
LEO... HEY..
GONNA KILL TODD.
PAOLO..
THIS IS 'EM.. AWKWARD, NO?

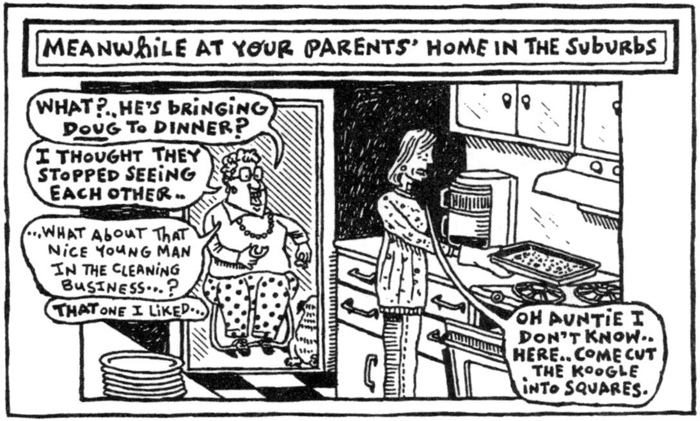
MEANWHILE AT YOUR PARENTS' HOME IN THE SUBURBS
WHAT?.. HE'S BRINGING DOUG TO DINNER?
I THOUGHT THEY STOPPED SEEING EACH OTHER..
...WHAT ABOUT THAT NICE YOUNG MAN IN THE CLEANING BUSINESS...?
THAT ONE I LIKED..
OH AUNTIE I DON'T KNOW.. HERE.. COME CUT THE KOOGLE INTO SQUARES.

end.

MEET MRS. GREEN...

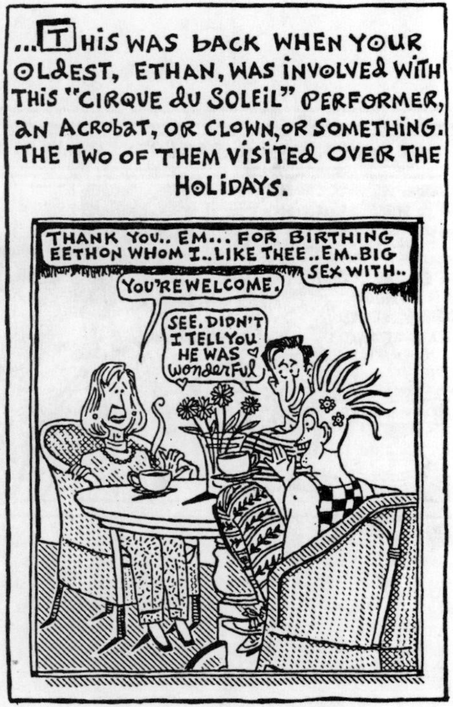
...THIS WAS BACK WHEN YOUR OLDEST, ETHAN, WAS INVOLVED WITH THIS "CIRQUE DU SOLEIL" PERFORMER, AN ACROBAT, OR CLOWN, OR SOMETHING. THE TWO OF THEM VISITED OVER THE HOLIDAYS.
THANK YOU.. EM... FOR BIRTHING EETHON WHOM I.. LIKE THEE.. EM.. BIG SEX WITH..
YOU'RE WELCOME.
SEE, DIDN'T I TELL YOU HE WAS wonderful

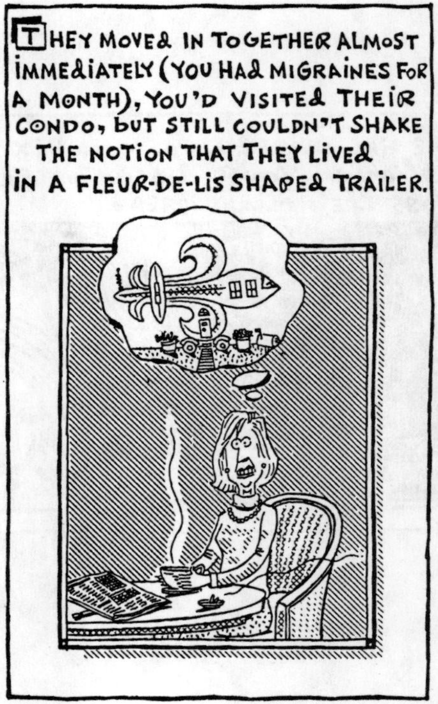
THEY MOVED IN TOGETHER ALMOST IMMEDIATELY (YOU HAD MIGRAINES FOR A MONTH), YOU'D VISITED THEIR CONDO, BUT STILL COULDN'T SHAKE THE NOTION THAT THEY LIVED IN A FLEUR-DE-LIS SHAPED TRAILER.

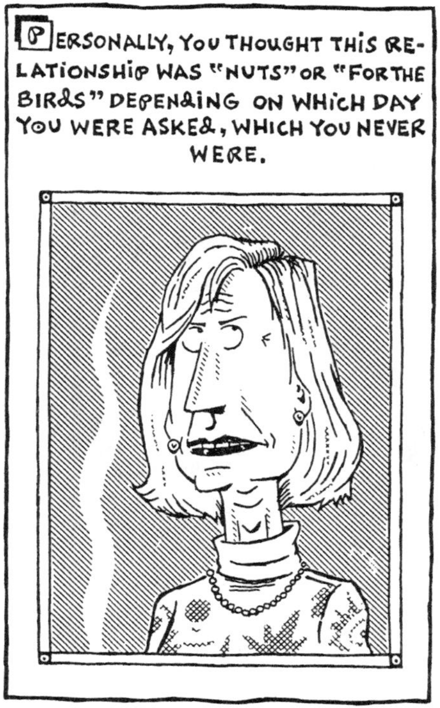
PERSONALLY, YOU THOUGHT THIS RELATIONSHIP WAS "NUTS" OR "FOR THE BIRDS" DEPENDING ON WHICH DAY YOU WERE ASKED, WHICH YOU NEVER WERE.

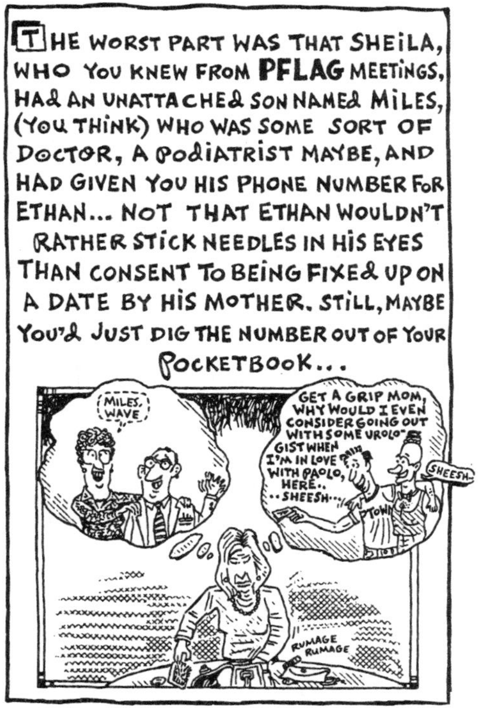
THE WORST PART WAS THAT SHEILA, WHO YOU KNEW FROM PFLAG MEETINGS, HAD AN UNATTACHED SON NAMED MILES, (YOU THINK) WHO WAS SOME SORT OF DOCTOR, A PODIATRIST MAYBE, AND HAD GIVEN YOU HIS PHONE NUMBER FOR ETHAN... NOT THAT ETHAN WOULDN'T RATHER STICK NEEDLES IN HIS EYES THAN CONSENT TO BEING FIXED UP ON A DATE BY HIS MOTHER. STILL, MAYBE YOU'D JUST DIG THE NUMBER OUT OF YOUR POCKETBOOK...
MILES, WAVE
GET A GRIP MOM, WHY WOULD I EVEN CONSIDER GOING OUT WITH SOME UROLOGIST WHEN I'M IN LOVE WITH PAOLO, HERE.. ..SHEESH...
SHEESH
PTOWN
RUMAGE RUMAGE

end.

GENTLEMEN SWALLOW YOUR BITTER PILLS.

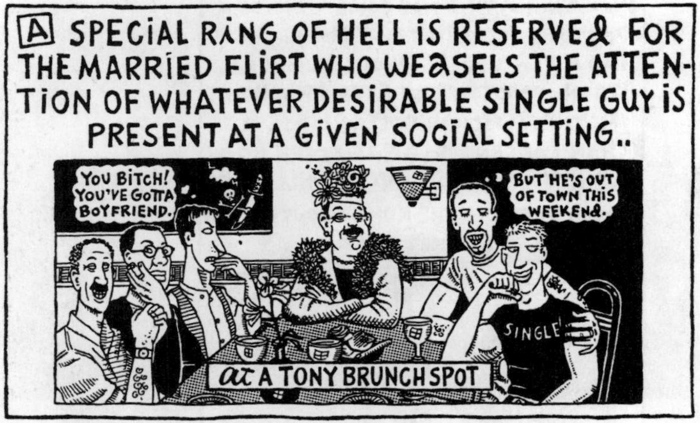
A SPECIAL RING OF HELL IS RESERVED FOR THE MARRIED FLIRT WHO WEASELS THE ATTENTION OF WHATEVER DESIRABLE SINGLE GUY IS PRESENT AT A GIVEN SOCIAL SETTING..
YOU BITCH! YOU'VE GOTTA BOYFRIEND.
BUT HE'S OUT OF TOWN THIS WEEKEND.
SINGLE
at A TONY BRUNCH SPOT

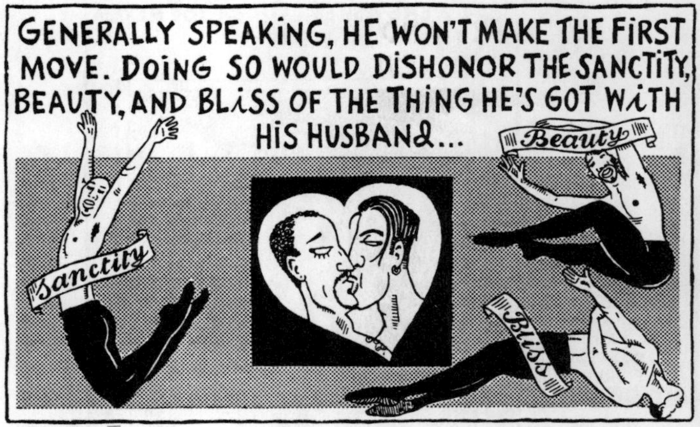
GENERALLY SPEAKING, HE WON'T MAKE THE FIRST MOVE. DOING SO WOULD DISHONOR THE SANCTITY, BEAUTY, AND BLISS OF THE THING HE'S GOT WITH HIS HUSBAND...
Sanctity
Beauty
Bliss

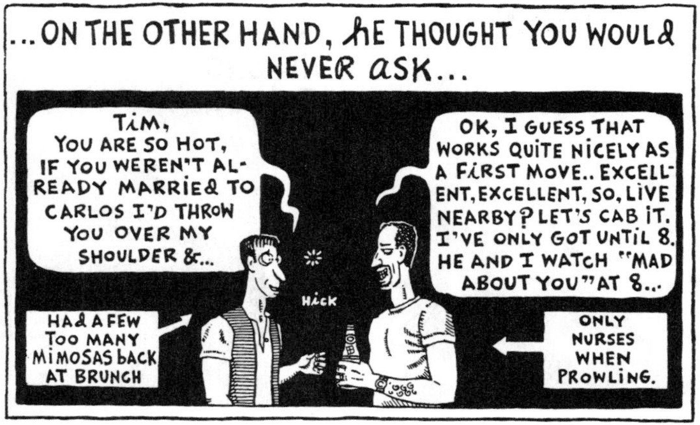
...ON THE OTHER HAND, HE THOUGHT YOU WOULD NEVER ASK...
TIM, YOU ARE SO HOT, IF YOU WEREN'T ALREADY MARRIED TO CARLOS I'D THROW YOU OVER MY SHOULDER &...
HICK
OK, I GUESS THAT WORKS QUITE NICELY AS A FIRST MOVE.. EXCELLENT, EXCELLENT, SO, LIVE NEARBY? LET'S CAB IT. I'VE ONLY GOT UNTIL 8. HE AND I WATCH "MAD ABOUT YOU" AT 8...
HAD A FEW TOO MANY MIMOSAS BACK AT BRUNCH
ONLY NURSES WHEN PROWLING.

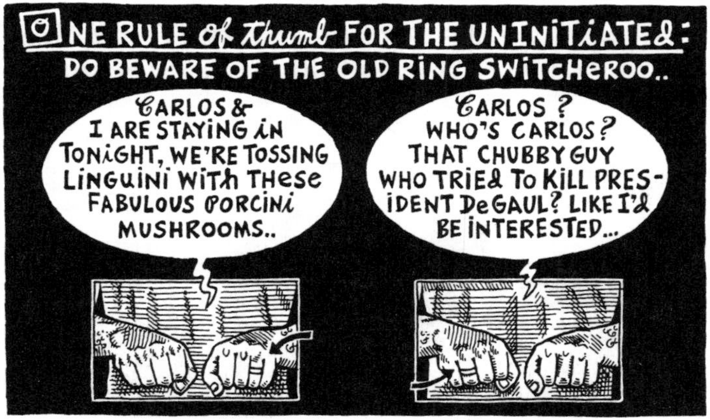
ONE RULE of thumb FOR THE UNINITIATED:
DO BEWARE OF THE OLD RING SWITCHEROO..
CARLOS & I ARE STAYING IN TONIGHT, WE'RE TOSSING LINGUINI WITH THESE FABULOUS PORCINI MUSHROOMS..
CARLOS? WHO'S CARLOS? THAT CHUBBY GUY WHO TRIED TO KILL PRESIDENT DeGAUL? LIKE I'D BE INTERESTED...

Continued...

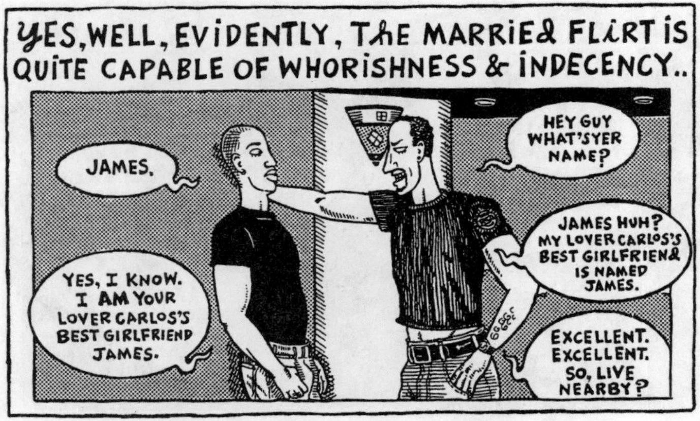
YES, WELL, EVIDENTLY, THE MARRIED FLIRT IS QUITE CAPABLE OF WHORISHNESS & INDECENCY..
HEY GUY WHAT'SYER NAME?
JAMES.
JAMES HUH? MY LOVER CARLOS'S BEST GIRLFRIEND IS NAMED JAMES.
YES, I KNOW. I AM YOUR LOVER CARLOS'S BEST GIRLFRIEND JAMES.
EXCELLENT. EXCELLENT. SO, LIVE NEARBY?

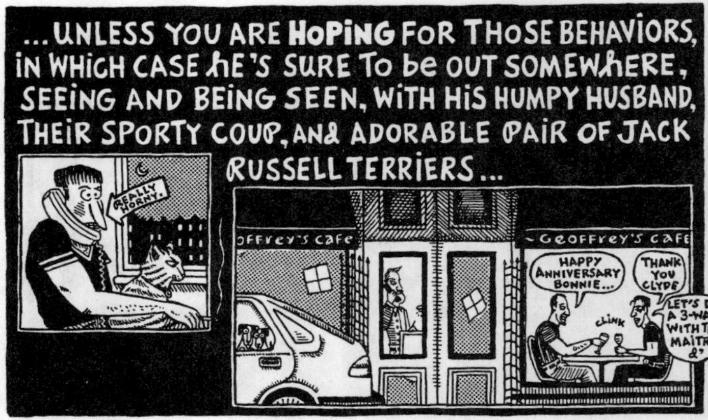
...UNLESS YOU ARE HOPING FOR THOSE BEHAVIORS, IN WHICH CASE HE'S SURE TO BE OUT SOMEWHERE, SEEING AND BEING SEEN, WITH HIS HUMPY HUSBAND, THEIR SPORTY COUP, AND ADORABLE PAIR OF JACK RUSSELL TERRIERS...
REALLY HORNY.
offrey's cafe
~Geoffrey's cafe
HAPPY ANNIVERSARY BONNIE...
THANK YOU CLYDE
CLINK
LET'S DO A 3-WAY WITH THE MAITRE D'

end.

A CONCERNED CHARLOTTE HAS PRIED THE NEARLY CATATONIC ETHAN FROM HIS LIVING ROOM SOFA, SITE OF THE RECENT SUSPENSION OF HIS ROMANCE WITH DOUG, FOR A CUP OF COFFEE AT THE NELLIE DELI...

SWEETHEART, I CAN HANDLE THE SLOPPY, "I'LL-NEVER-FALL-IN-LOVE-AGAIN" ETHAN, THE PEEVISH, EMBITTERED ETHAN, OR THE DESPARATELY & PATHETICALLY ABANDONED ETHAN. BUT THIS— THE ENTIRELY MOROSE ETHAN... WELL THIS I SIMPLY CANNOT STAND. YOU GOTTA **EMOTE** BABY, OR YOU'RE GONNA DRIVE ME INSANE! HERE... EAT SOME SCONE. C'MON, CHEW... SWALLOW...

Continued...

GIRL, WHEN'R YOU GONNA CHECK OUT OF **THAT** LOVE LIFE & CHECK INTO **THIS** ONE.

MEANWHILE, AT THE HOSPICE ACROSS TOWN;
I WILL NOT THINK ABOUT ETHAN, I WILL THINK ABOUT VOLUNTEERING. I WILL NOT THINK ABOUT ETHAN, I WILL THINK ABOUT VOLUNTEERING. I WILL NOT THINK
NELS

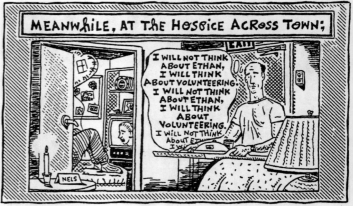

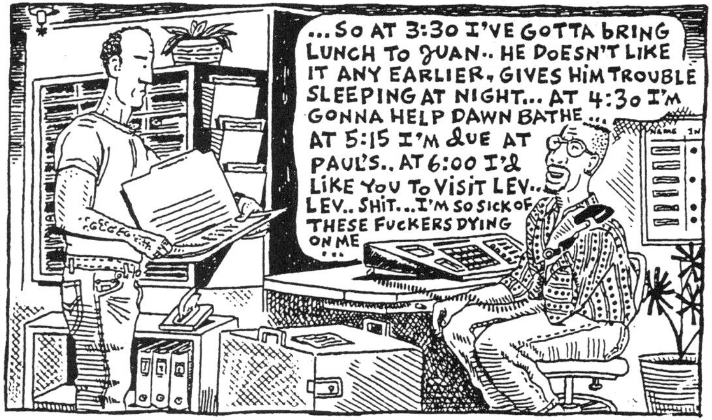
...SO AT 3:30 I'VE GOTTA BRING LUNCH TO JUAN.. HE DOESN'T LIKE IT ANY EARLIER, GIVES HIM TROUBLE SLEEPING AT NIGHT... AT 4:30 I'M GONNA HELP DAWN BATHE... AT 5:15 I'M DUE AT PAUL'S.. AT 6:00 I'D LIKE YOU TO VISIT LEV... LEV.. SHIT... I'M SO SICK OF THESE FUCKERS DYING ON ME ...

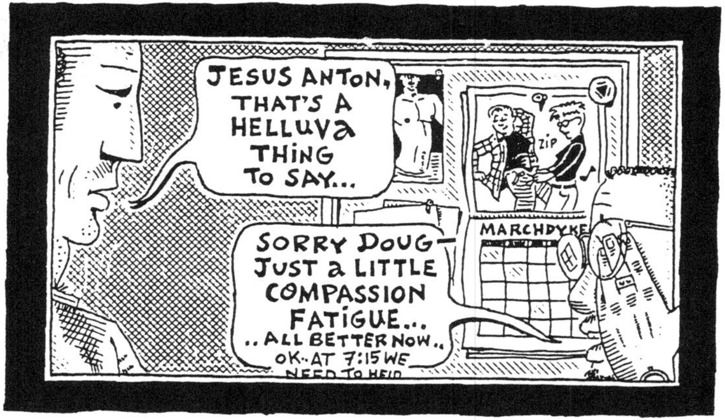
JESUS ANTON, THAT'S A HELLUVA THING TO SAY...
ZIP
MARCHDYKE
SORRY DOUG—JUST A LITTLE COMPASSION FATIGUE... ..ALL BETTER NOW.. OK.. AT 7:15 WE

end.

TIME TRAVELIN' SISTERS

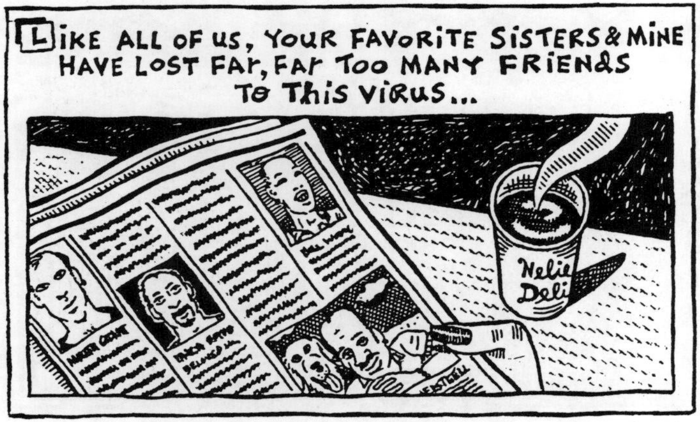
LIKE ALL OF US, YOUR FAVORITE SISTERS & MINE HAVE LOST FAR, FAR TOO MANY FRIENDS TO THIS VIRUS...
Nelie Deli

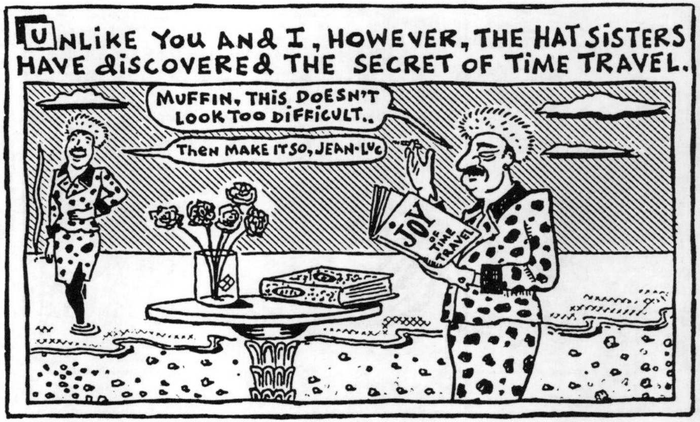
UNLIKE YOU AND I, HOWEVER, THE HAT SISTERS HAVE DISCOVERED THE SECRET OF TIME TRAVEL.
MUFFIN, THIS DOESN'T LOOK TOO DIFFICULT..
Then MAKE IT SO, JEAN-LUC
JOY OF TIME TRAVEL

WHY, JUST LAST SATURDAY AFTERNOON, THE GALS TOOK AN EXTRA BIG BOX OF CONDOMS BACK TO 1978...

THEIR MISSION: SHEATH THOSE THEY'VE LOST BEFORE FLUID EXCHANGE.

Continued...

DUE TO THE NUMBER OF STOPS THEY NEEDED TO MAKE, GENTLE PERSUASION WAS ABANDONED.

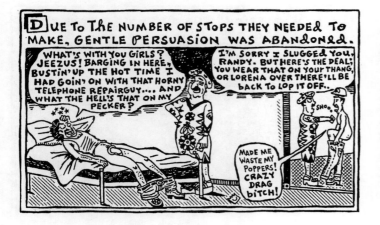

WHAT'S WITH YOU GIRLS? JEEZUS! BARGING IN HERE, BUSTIN' UP THE HOT TIME I HAD GOIN' ON WITH THAT HORNY TELEPHONE REPAIRGUY.... AND WHAT THE HELL'S THAT ON MY PECKER?

I'M SORRY I SLUGGED YOU, RANDY. BUT HERE'S THE DEAL: YOU WEAR THAT ON YOUR THANG, OR LORENA OVER THERE'LL BE BACK TO LOP IT OFF..

SHOO..

MADE ME WASTE MY POPPERS! CRAZY DRAG BITCH!

'COURSE TIME TRAVEL IS A TRICKY BUSINESS, SINCE ANY DISRUPTION IN THE TIME-SPACE CONTINUUM HAS A "RIPPLE" EFFECT, ALTERING REALITY IN OUR OWN TIME. WHICH AIN'T ALL BAD, SOMETIMES.

PRESIDENT ROSEANNE BARR SIGNS NAT'L HEALTH INSURANCE BILL INTO LAW.

KHAIR OF JOINT CHIEFS JOE STEFFAN BRIEFS NATION ON HAITI.

"WE KICKED SOME REACTIONARY BUTT!"

P'TOWN CLOSED TO STRAIGHT TOURISTS FROM HYANNIS

Bean O QUEEN

end.

CELIBATE IN THE LONG WEEKS SINCE YOUR "TIME OUT" WITH DOUG, AND HAVING NOT QUITE MET THAT LEVEL OF DESPERATION WHICH COMPELS MEN TO VISIT THEIR *local* SEX CLUB, YOU COMPROMISE WITH YOUR INSISTENT LIBIDO BY SHOWING UP AT A BATHHOUSE *out of town*...

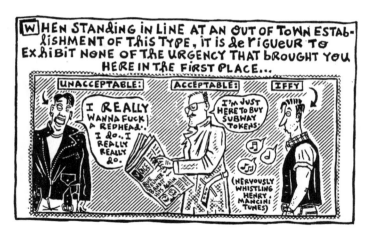

WHEN STANDING IN LINE AT AN OUT OF TOWN ESTABLISHMENT OF THIS TYPE, IT IS *de rigueur* TO EXHIBIT NONE OF THE URGENCY THAT BROUGHT YOU HERE IN THE FIRST PLACE...

UNACCEPTABLE:

I REALLY WANNA FUCK A REDHEAD. I DO... I REALLY REALLY DO.

ACCEPTABLE:

I'M JUST HERE TO BUY SUBWAY TOKENS.

IFFY

(NERVOUSLY WHISTLING HENRY MANCINI TUNES)

Continued...

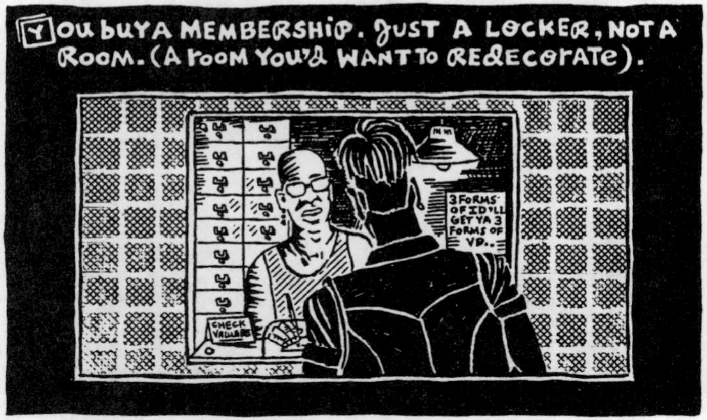
YOU BUY A MEMBERSHIP. JUST A LOCKER, NOT A ROOM. (A ROOM YOU'D WANT TO REDECORATE).
3 FORMS OF ID'LL GET YA 3 FORMS OF VD..
CHECK VALUABLES

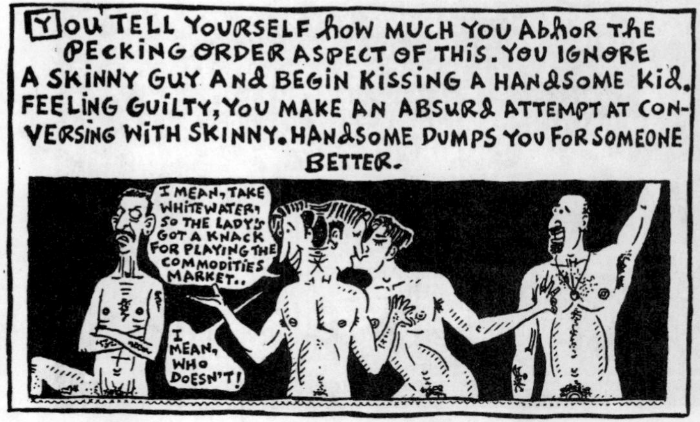
YOU TELL YOURSELF HOW MUCH YOU ABHOR THE PECKING ORDER ASPECT OF THIS. YOU IGNORE A SKINNY GUY AND BEGIN KISSING A HANDSOME KID. FEELING GUILTY, YOU MAKE AN ABSURD ATTEMPT AT CONVERSING WITH SKINNY. HANDSOME DUMPS YOU FOR SOMEONE BETTER.
I MEAN, TAKE WHITEWATER, SO THE LADY'S GOT A KNACK FOR PLAYING THE COMMODITIES MARKET..
I MEAN, WHO DOESN'T!

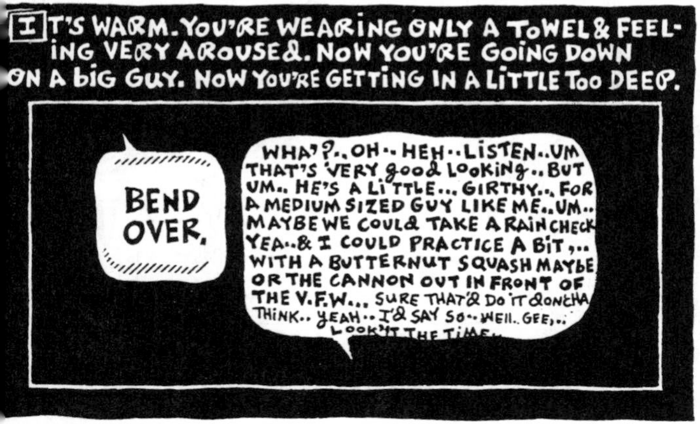
IT'S WARM. YOU'RE WEARING ONLY A TOWEL & FEELING VERY AROUSED. NOW YOU'RE GOING DOWN ON A BIG GUY. NOW YOU'RE GETTING IN A LITTLE TOO DEEP.
BEND OVER.
WHA'?.. OH.. HEH.. LISTEN.. UM THAT'S VERY GOOD LOOKING.. BUT UM.. HE'S A LITTLE... GIRTHY.., FOR A MEDIUM SIZED GUY LIKE ME.. UM.. MAYBE WE COULD TAKE A RAINCHECK YEA.. & I COULD PRACTICE A BIT,.. WITH A BUTTERNUT SQUASH MAYBE OR THE CANNON OUT IN FRONT OF THE V.F.W... SURE THAT'D DO IT DONCHA THINK.. YEAH.. I'D SAY SO.. WELL.. GEE,..

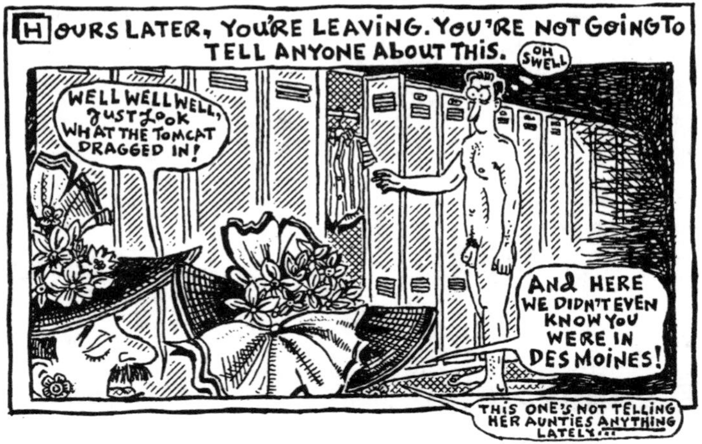
HOURS LATER, YOU'RE LEAVING. YOU'RE NOT GOING TO TELL ANYONE ABOUT THIS.
OH SWELL
WELL WELL WELL, JUST LOOK WHAT THE TOMCAT DRAGGED IN!
AND HERE WE DIDN'T EVEN KNOW YOU WERE IN DES MOINES!
THIS ONE'S NOT TELLING HER AUNTIES ANYTHING LATELY...

end.

THE EXPLANATION.

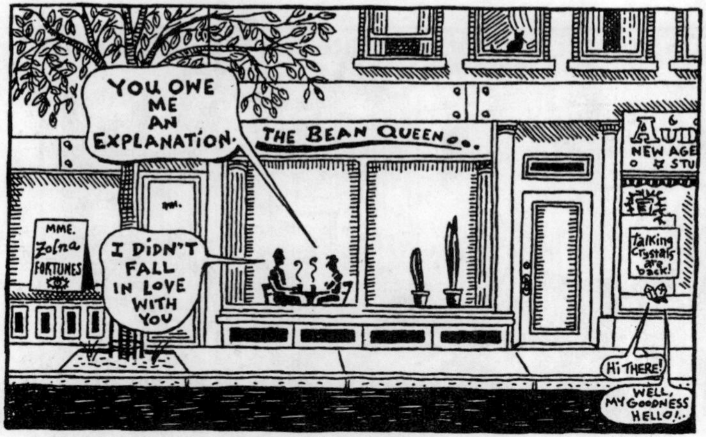
YOU OWE ME AN EXPLANATION.
THE BEAN QUEEN
MME. Zolna FORTUNES
I DIDN'T FALL IN LOVE WITH YOU
NEW AGE
Talking Crystals are back!
Hi THERE!
WELL, MY GOODNESS HELLO!

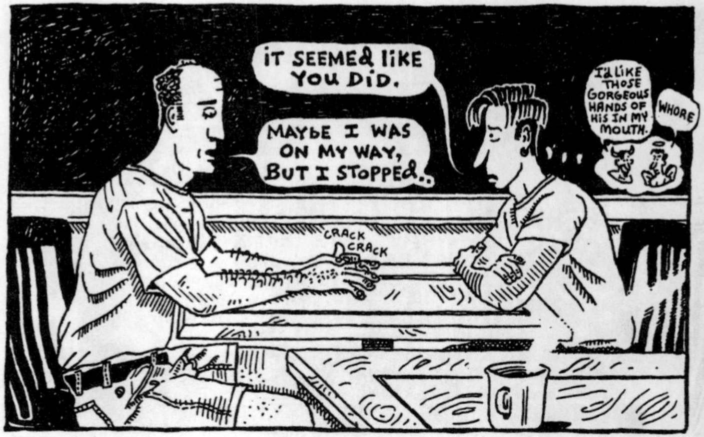
IT SEEMED LIKE YOU DID.
MAYBE I WAS ON MY WAY, BUT I STOPPED..
CRACK
CRACK
I'D LIKE THOSE GORGEOUS HANDS OF HIS IN MY MOUTH.
WHORE

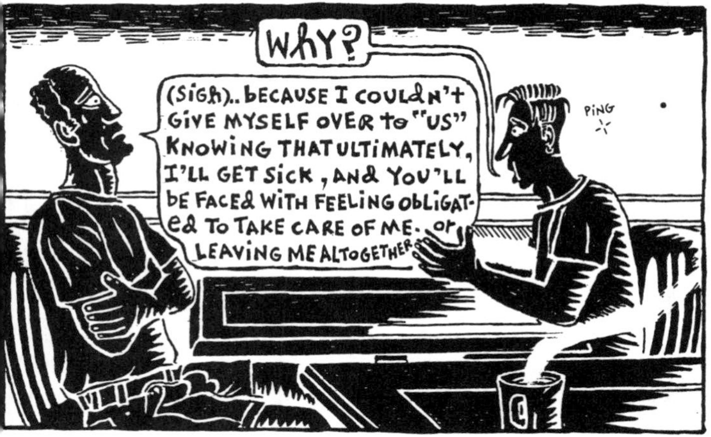
WHY?
(SIGH).. BECAUSE I COULDN'T GIVE MYSELF OVER TO "US" KNOWING THAT ULTIMATELY, I'LL GET SICK, AND YOU'LL BE FACED WITH FEELING OBLIGATED TO TAKE CARE OF ME.. OR LEAVING ME ALTOGETHER.
PING

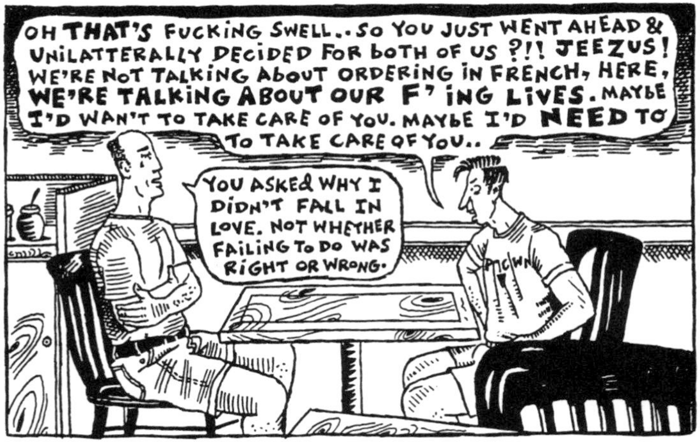
YOU ASKED WHY I DIDN'T FALL IN LOVE. NOT WHETHER FAILING TO DO WAS RIGHT OR WRONG.
OH THAT'S FUCKING SWELL.. SO YOU JUST WENT AHEAD & UNILATTERALLY DECIDED FOR BOTH OF US ?!! JEEZUS! WE'RE NOT TALKING ABOUT ORDERING IN FRENCH, HERE, WE'RE TALKING ABOUT OUR F' ING LIVES. MAYBE I'D WAN'T TO TAKE CARE OF YOU. MAYBE I'D NEED TO TO TAKE CARE OF YOU..

Continued...

HERE'S THE DEAL CONTROL QUEEN, IF YOU GET SICK, I'M THERE. INVITED OR NOT. I LOVE YOU.
SCRAPE
....I LOVE YOU TOO....
OH TERRIFIC! SO WHAT DOES THAT MAKE "US"?
KIND'A FUCKED, I GUESS..
OPEN

end.

WINTER MORNING.

IT'S THE DEAD OF WINTER. THE WARMER MONTHS ARE GONE, AND WITH THEM THEIR OPPORTUNITY FOR CHANCE ENCOUNTERS WITH MEN WHO WOULD BE YOUR LOVER.

SUMMERS ARE FOR BEING SINGLE. WINTERS ARE FOR SUNDAY MORNINGS AND HIM CLIMBING BACK INTO BED WITH THE PAPER.

Continued...

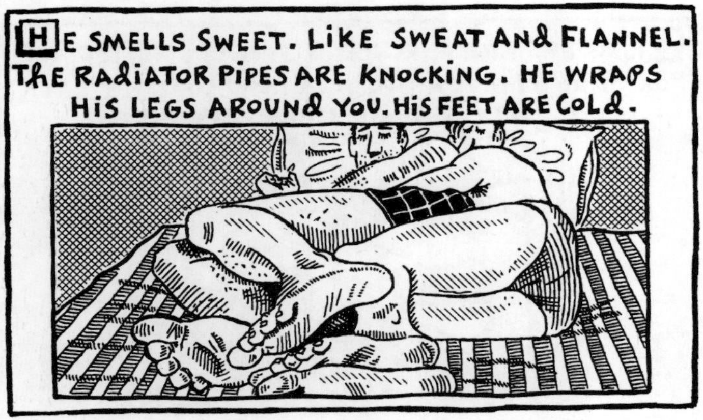
HE SMELLS SWEET. LIKE SWEAT AND FLANNEL. THE RADIATOR PIPES ARE KNOCKING. HE WRAPS HIS LEGS AROUND YOU. HIS FEET ARE COLD.

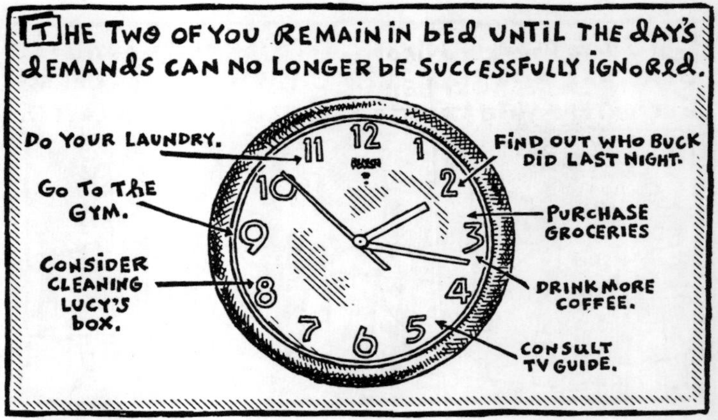
THE TWO OF YOU REMAIN IN BED UNTIL THE DAY'S DEMANDS CAN NO LONGER BE SUCCESSFULLY IGNORED.
DO YOUR LAUNDRY.
GO TO THE GYM.
CONSIDER CLEANING LUCY'S BOX.
FIND OUT WHO BUCK DID LAST NIGHT.
PURCHASE GROCERIES
DRINK MORE COFFEE.
CONSULT TV GUIDE.
12
1
2
3
4
5
6
7
8
9
10
11

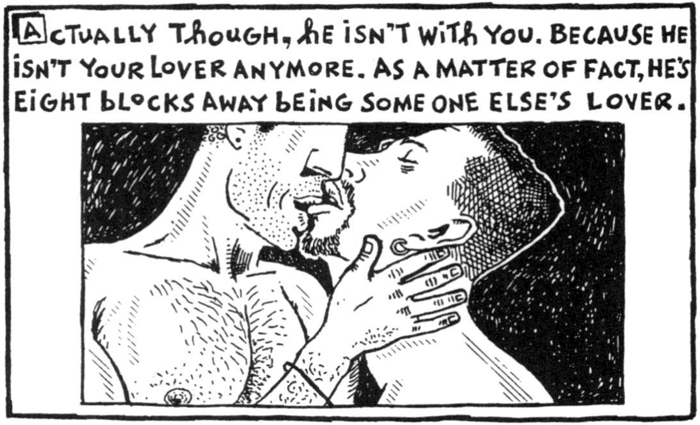
ACTUALLY THOUGH, HE ISN'T WITH YOU. BECAUSE HE ISN'T YOUR LOVER ANYMORE. AS A MATTER OF FACT, HE'S EIGHT BLOCKS AWAY BEING SOME ONE ELSE'S LOVER.

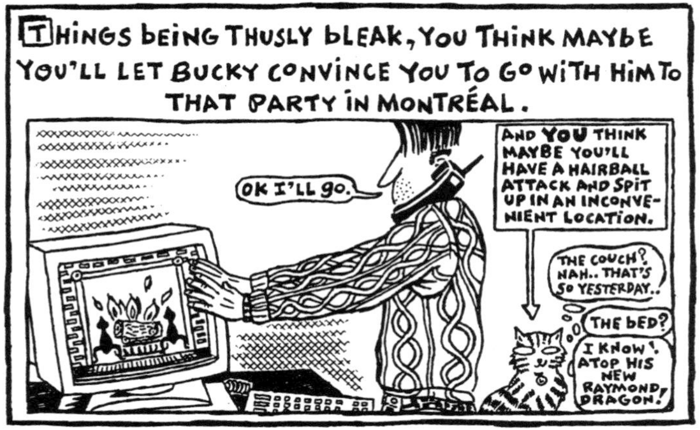
THINGS BEING THUSLY BLEAK, YOU THINK MAYBE YOU'LL LET BUCKY CONVINCE YOU TO GO WITH HIM TO THAT PARTY IN MONTRÉAL.
OK I'LL GO.
AND YOU THINK MAYBE YOU'LL HAVE A HAIRBALL ATTACK AND SPIT UP IN AN INCONVENIENT LOCATION.
THE COUCH? NAH.. THAT'S SO YESTERDAY..
THE BED?
I KNOW! ATOP HIS NEW RAYMOND DRAGON!

end.

ROAD TRIPPING WITH BUCKY.

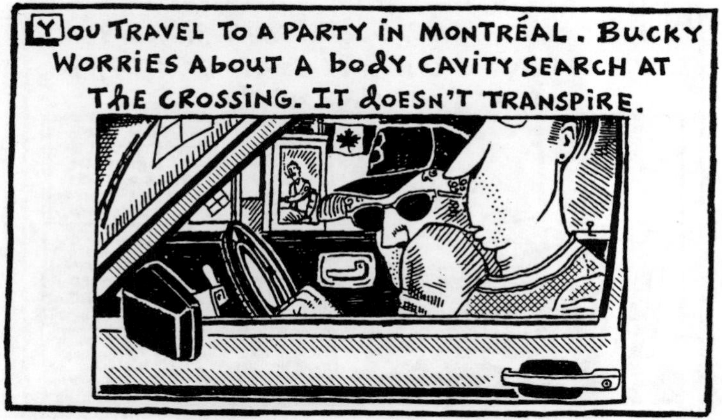
YOU TRAVEL TO A PARTY IN MONTRÉAL. BUCKY WORRIES ABOUT A BODY CAVITY SEARCH AT THE CROSSING. IT DOESN'T TRANSPIRE.

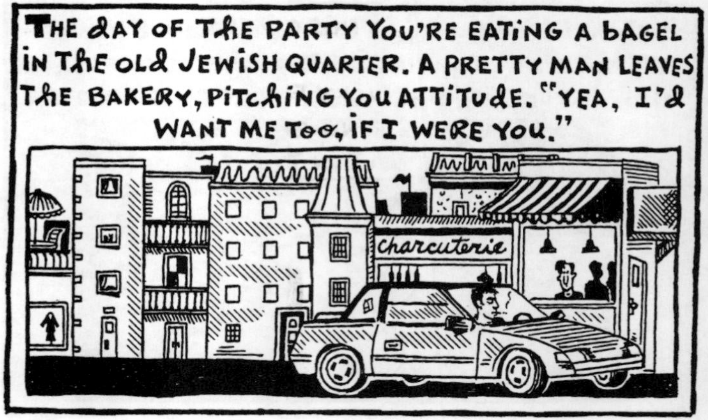
THE DAY OF THE PARTY YOU'RE EATING A BAGEL IN THE OLD JEWISH QUARTER. A PRETTY MAN LEAVES THE BAKERY, PITCHING YOU ATTITUDE. "YEA, I'D WANT ME TOO, IF I WERE YOU."
charcuterie

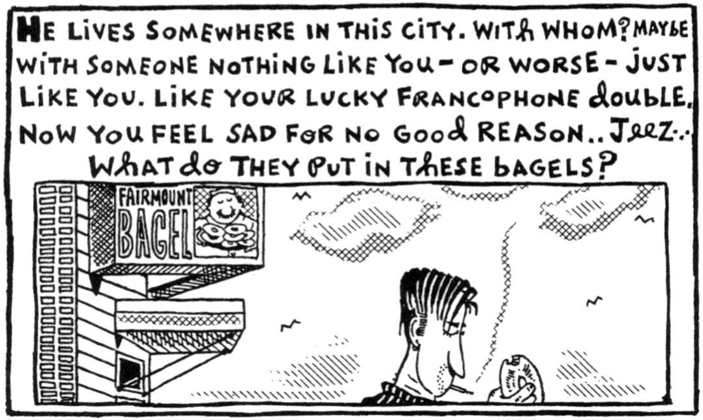
HE LIVES SOMEWHERE IN THIS CITY. WITH WHOM? MAYBE WITH SOMEONE NOTHING LIKE YOU - OR WORSE - JUST LIKE YOU. LIKE YOUR LUCKY FRANCOPHONE DOUBLE. NOW YOU FEEL SAD FOR NO GOOD REASON.. JEEZ.. WHAT DO THEY PUT IN THESE BAGELS?
FAIRMOUNT
BAGEL

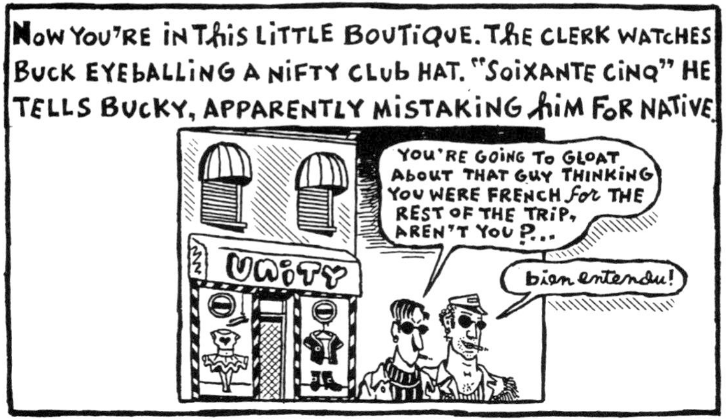
NOW YOU'RE IN THIS LITTLE BOUTIQUE. THE CLERK WATCHES BUCK EYEBALLING A NIFTY CLUB HAT. "SOIXANTE CINQ" HE TELLS BUCKY, APPARENTLY MISTAKING HIM FOR NATIVE.
UNITY
YOU'RE GOING TO GLOAT ABOUT THAT GUY THINKING YOU WERE FRENCH FOR THE REST OF THE TRIP, AREN'T YOU?..
bien entendu!

Continued...

BUCKY, WHO YOU HAVEN'T SEEN OUT OF TIMBERLANDS IN YEARS, HAS ABRUPTLY GONE EURO, AND IS SPORTING THESE INTIMIDATING, POINTY "JOHN FLUEVOGS".

THE TWO OF YOU DO THE OBLIGATORY PRE-PARTY WORK OUT. YOU SCAN THE GLITZY GYM FOR ETIENNE. UNSUCCESSFULLY.

end.

ON THE CIRCUIT.

T|HE CIRCUIT PARTY IS HUGE ANd JARRING AND DISSONANT. BUCK TELLS YOU THAT THIS WILL CHANGE WHEN SOMEONE CALLED JUNIOR STARTS PLAYING.

Y|OU ARE BEING PULLED INTO A BETTER MOOD. THINGS ARE GETTING MORE EVEN. RHYTHMIC.

Continued...

There are people here without party invitations, but they're not very popular.

You're dancing with these guys you've seen at home, but never spoken to. Your eyes are sharing intimate, unspoken confidences.

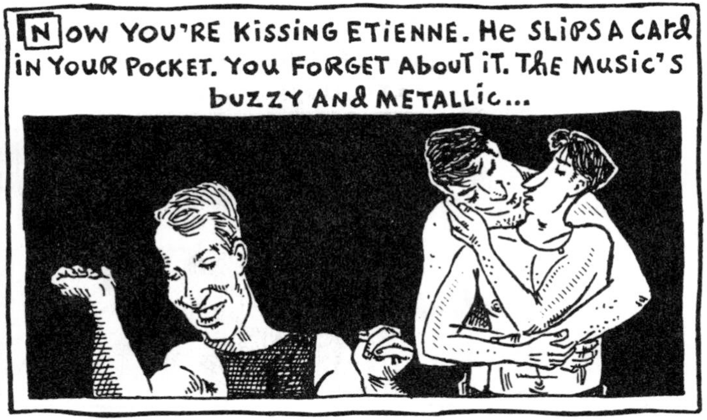
NOW YOU'RE KISSING ETIENNE. HE SLIPS A CARD IN YOUR POCKET. YOU FORGET ABOUT IT. THE MUSIC'S BUZZY AND METALLIC...

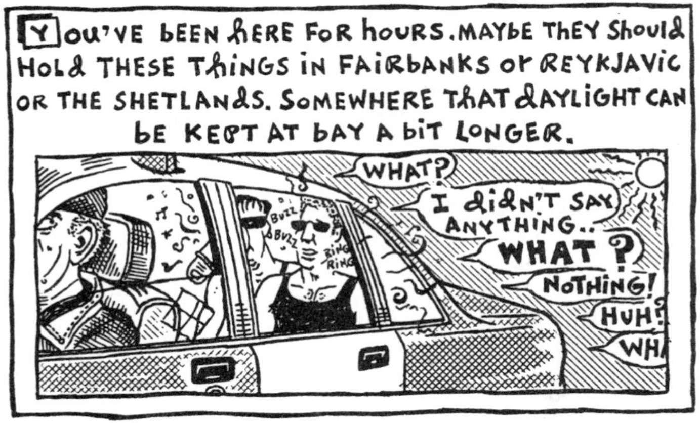
YOU'VE BEEN HERE FOR HOURS. MAYBE THEY SHOULD HOLD THESE THINGS IN FAIRBANKS OR REYKJAVIC OR THE SHETLANDS. SOMEWHERE THAT DAYLIGHT CAN BE KEPT AT BAY A BIT LONGER.
WHAT?
I DIDN'T SAY ANYTHING..
WHAT?
NOTHING!
HUH!?
WH
BUZZ BUZZ
RING RING

end.

AU MONTRÉAL.

YOU FIND A CARD FROM ETIENNE IN YOUR JEANS. HE MUST'VE GIVEN IT TO YOU AT THE PARTY. YOU CAN'T REMEMBER.
OVERALL POST-PARTY LOVELINESS
GROAN
IT TURNS OUT HE'S SOME SORT OF CELEBRATED CHEF AT A CUTTING EDGE BISTRO ON ST. DENIS.
ETTIENNE
204

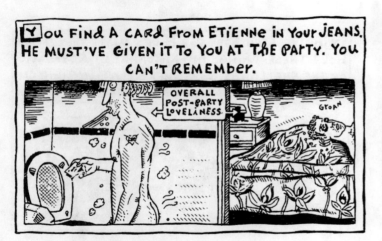

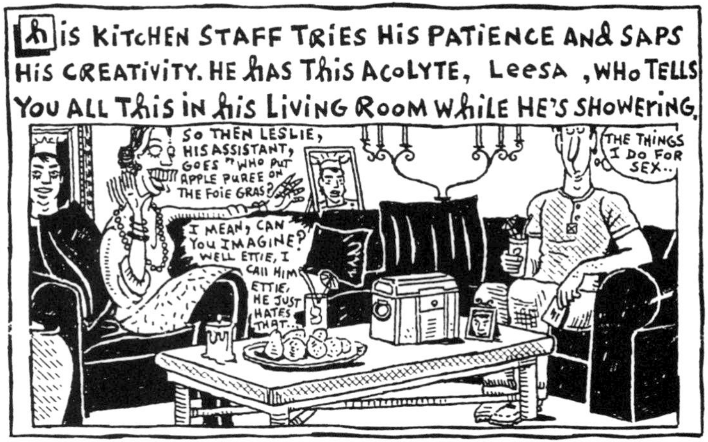
HIS KITCHEN STAFF TRIES HIS PATIENCE AND SAPS HIS CREATIVITY. HE HAS THIS ACOLYTE, LEESA, WHO TELLS YOU ALL THIS IN HIS LIVING ROOM WHILE HE'S SHOWERING.
SO THEN LESLIE, HIS ASSISTANT, GOES "WHO PUT APPLE PUREE ON THE FOIE GRAS?"
I MEAN, CAN YOU IMAGINE? WELL ETTIE, I CALL HIM ETTIE, HE JUST HATES THAT...
THE THINGS I DO FOR SEX...

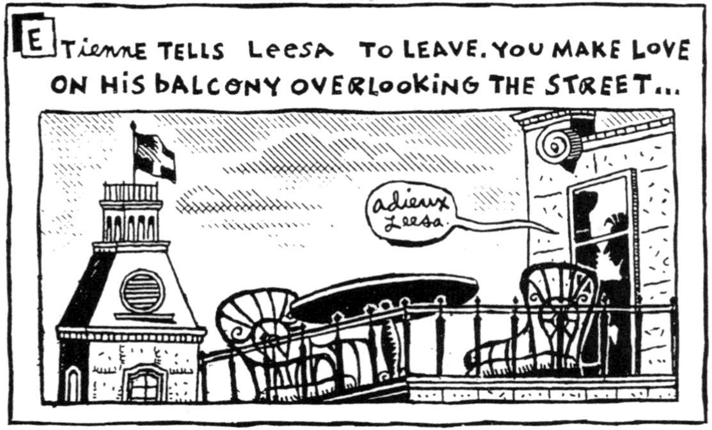
ETIENNE TELLS LEESA TO LEAVE. YOU MAKE LOVE ON HIS BALCONY OVERLOOKING THE STREET...
adieux Leesa.

Continued...

This is an intoxicating place. You wonder if they let Americans work here. Given the last election, you wonder if they let Americans live here.

BY ALL MEANS, GO... TAKE MY KID SISTER WITH YOU.

Leesa's buzzing from downstairs. It's 4 pm and Etienne's due at the restaurant— (apparently she drives him)—he tells you to stay in bed and wait for him. You do as you are told.

end.

THE ETHAN GREEN GUIDE TO CRUISING.

by Eric Orner.

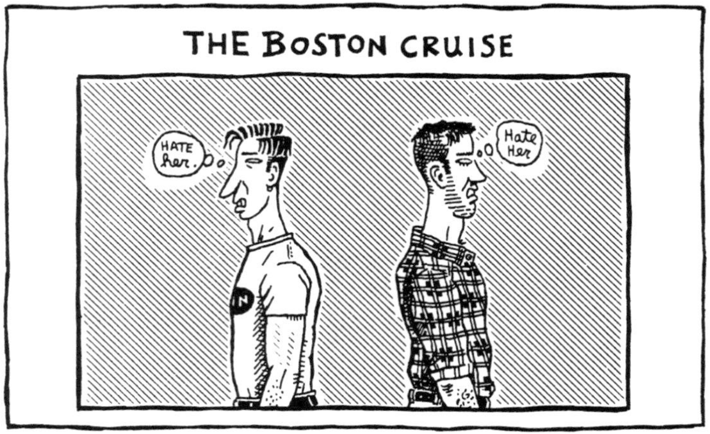
THE BOSTON CRUISE
HATE her.
Hate Her

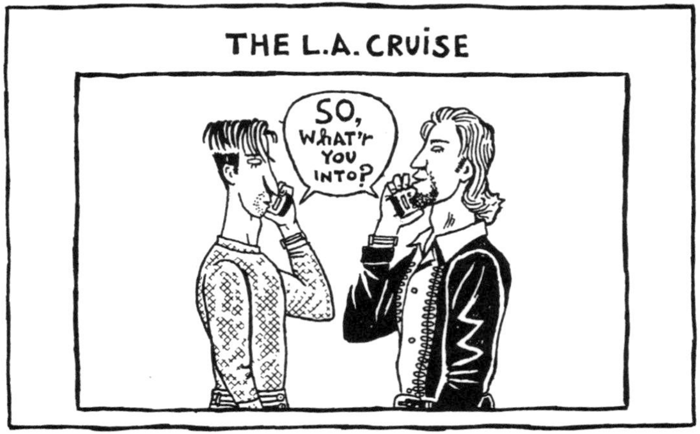
THE L.A. CRUISE
SO, WHAT'r YOU INTO?

Continued...

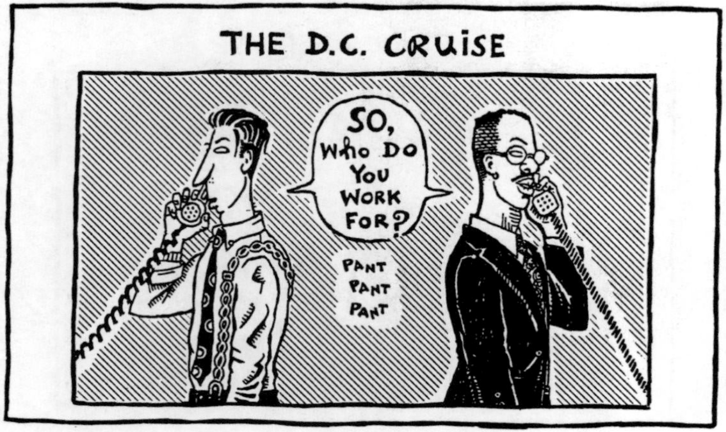
THE D.C. CRUISE
SO, WHO DO YOU WORK FOR?
PANT PANT PANT

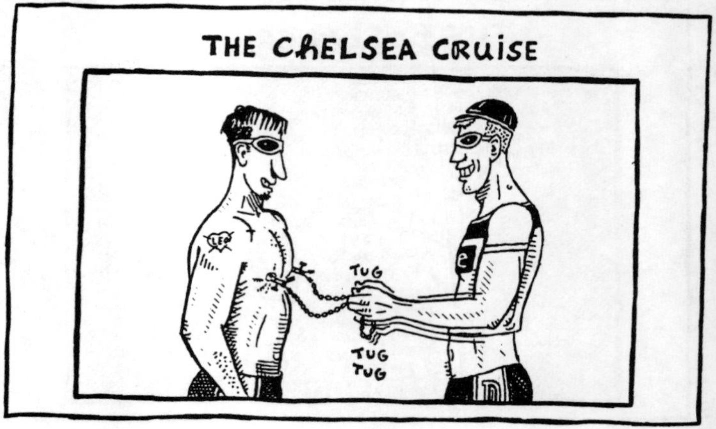
THE CHELSEA CRUISE
TUG
TUG TUG

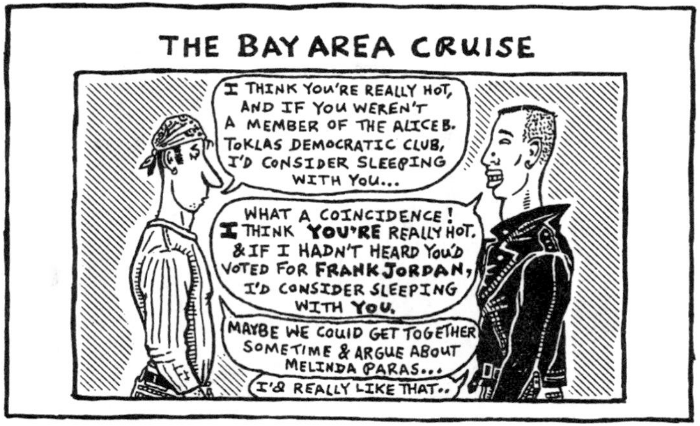
THE BAY AREA CRUISE
I THINK YOU'RE REALLY HOT, AND IF YOU WEREN'T A MEMBER OF THE ALICE B. TOKLAS DEMOCRATIC CLUB, I'D CONSIDER SLEEPING WITH YOU...
WHAT A COINCIDENCE! I THINK YOU'RE REALLY HOT. & IF I HADN'T HEARD YOU'D VOTED FOR FRANK JORDAN, I'D CONSIDER SLEEPING WITH YOU.
MAYBE WE COULD GET TOGETHER SOMETIME & ARGUE ABOUT MELINDA PARAS...
I'D REALLY LIKE THAT..

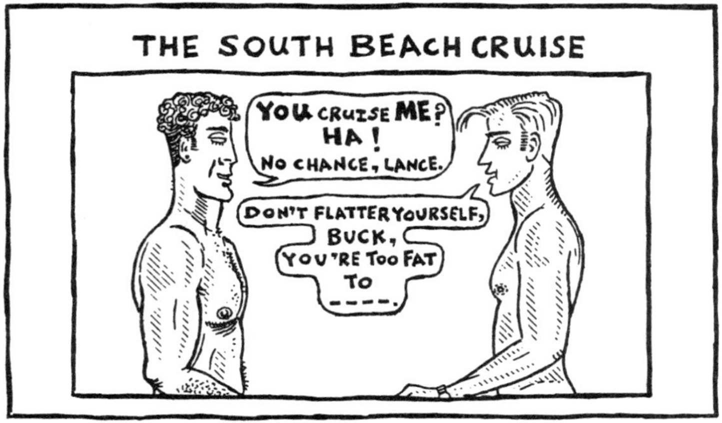
THE SOUTH BEACH CRUISE
YOU CRUISE ME? HA! NO CHANCE, LANCE.
DON'T FLATTER YOURSELF, BUCK, YOU'RE TOO FAT TO ----.

Continued...

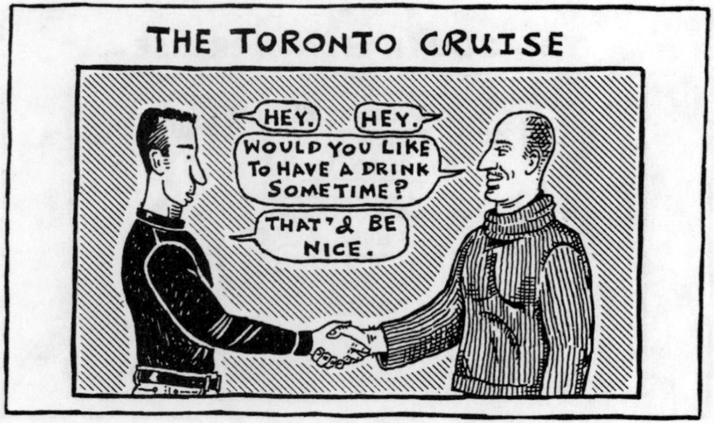
THE TORONTO CRUISE
HEY.
HEY.
WOULD YOU LIKE TO HAVE A DRINK SOMETIME?
THAT'D BE NICE.

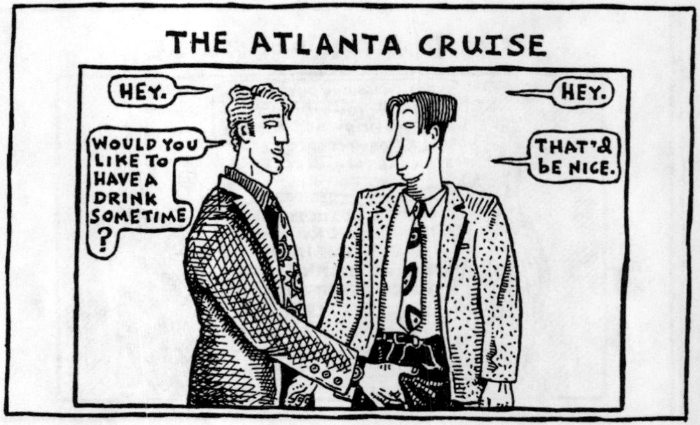
THE ATLANTA CRUISE
HEY.
HEY.
WOULD YOU LIKE TO HAVE A DRINK SOMETIME?
THAT'D BE NICE.

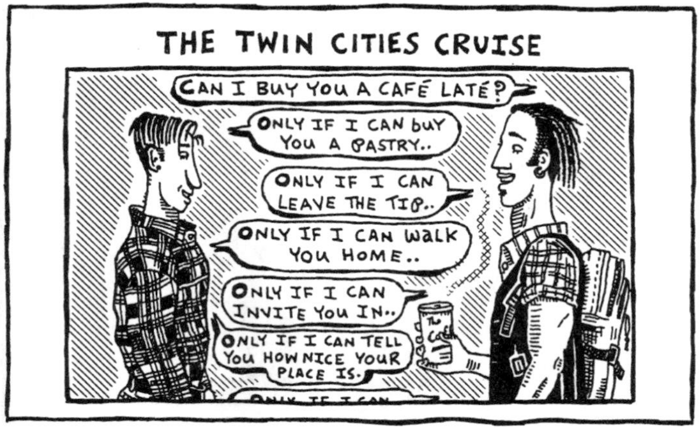
THE TWIN CITIES CRUISE
CAN I BUY YOU A CAFÉ LATÉ?
ONLY IF I CAN BUY YOU A PASTRY..
ONLY IF I CAN LEAVE THE TIP..
ONLY IF I CAN WALK YOU HOME..
ONLY IF I CAN INVITE YOU IN..
ONLY IF I CAN TELL YOU HOW NICE YOUR PLACE IS.

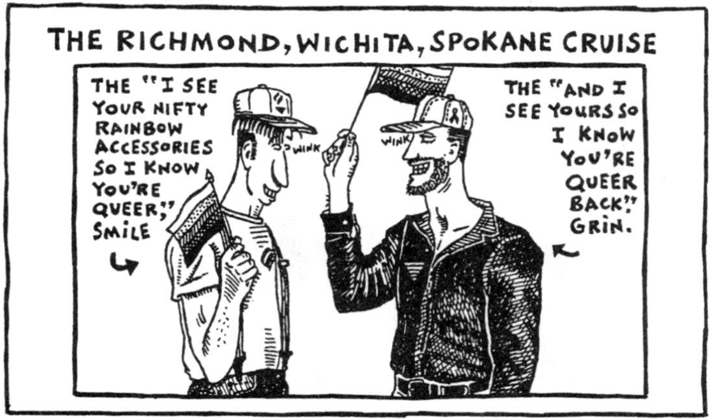
THE RICHMOND, WICHITA, SPOKANE CRUISE
THE "I SEE YOUR NIFTY RAINBOW ACCESSORIES SO I KNOW YOU'RE QUEER," SMILE
WINK
WINK
THE "AND I SEE YOURS SO I KNOW YOU'RE QUEER BACK," GRIN.

Continued...

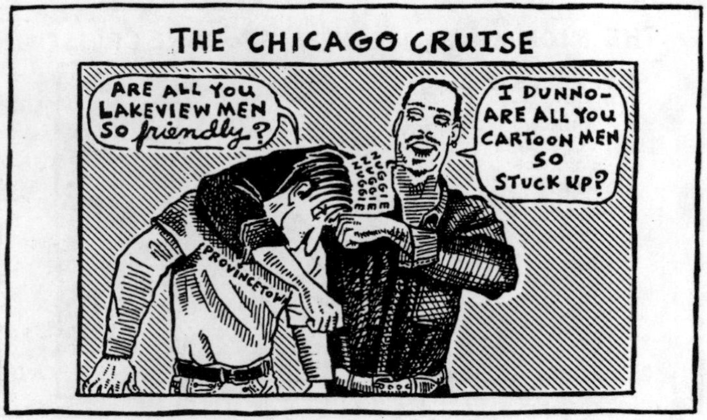
THE CHICAGO CRUISE
ARE ALL YOU LAKEVIEW MEN SO *friendly*?
I DUNNO- ARE ALL YOU CARTOON MEN SO STUCK UP?
NUGGIE NUGGIE NUGGIE
PROVINCETOWN

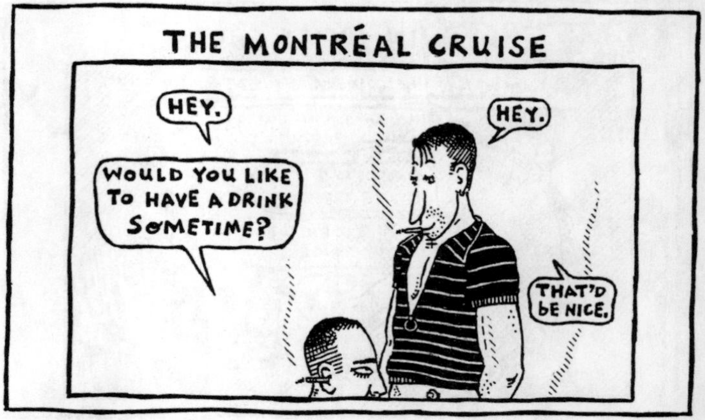
THE MONTRÉAL CRUISE
HEY.
HEY.
WOULD YOU LIKE TO HAVE A DRINK SOMETIME?
THAT'D BE NICE.

end.

Valentines Day Massacres...

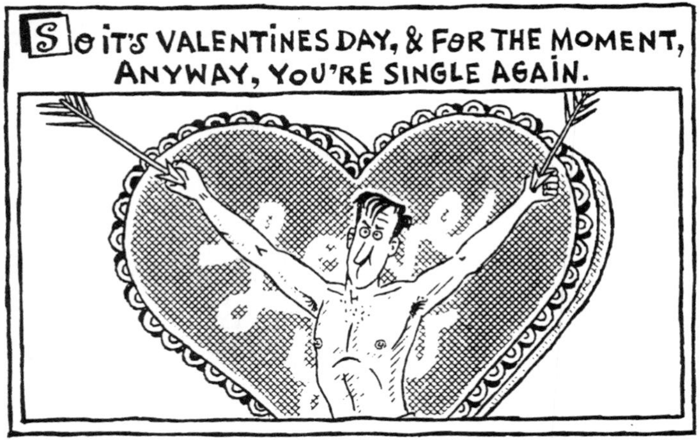

SO IT'S VALENTINES DAY, & FOR THE MOMENT, ANYWAY, YOU'RE SINGLE AGAIN.

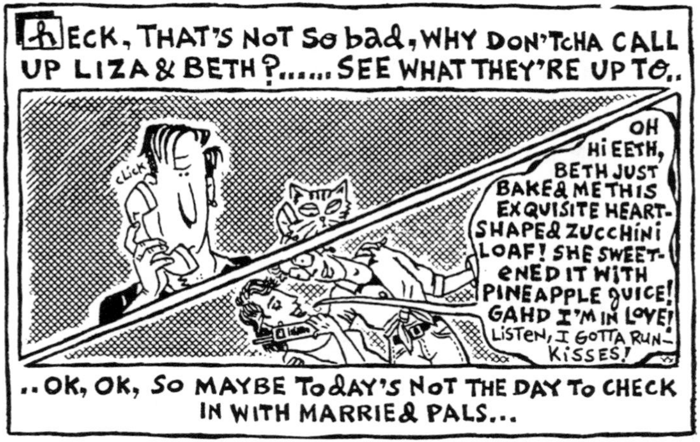

HECK, THAT'S NOT SO BAD, WHY DON'TCHA CALL UP LIZA & BETH?...... SEE WHAT THEY'RE UP TO..
CLICK
OH HI EETH, BETH JUST BAKED ME THIS EXQUISITE HEART-SHAPED ZUCCHINI LOAF! SHE SWEETENED IT WITH PINEAPPLE JUICE! GAHD I'M IN LOVE! LISTEN, I GOTTA RUN- KISSES!
..OK, OK, SO MAYBE TODAY'S NOT THE DAY TO CHECK IN WITH MARRIED PALS...

Continued...

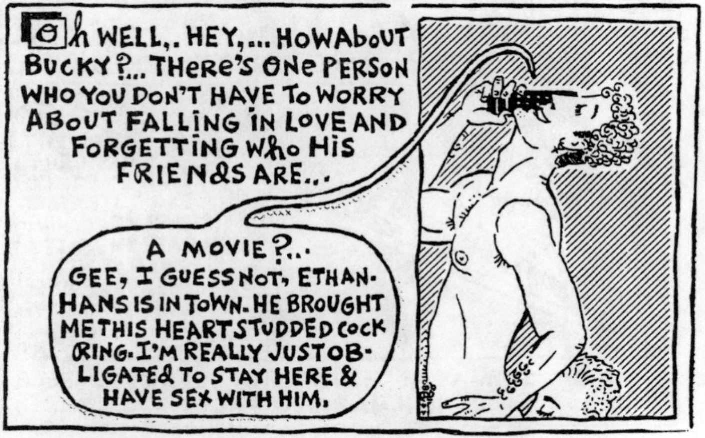
Oh WELL,. HEY,... HOWAbout BUCKY?... THere's ONe PERSON WHO YOU DON'T HAVE To WORRY ABout FALLING IN LOVE AND FORGETTING Who HIS FRIENDS ARE...
A MOVIE?.. GEE, I GUESS NOT, ETHAN. HANS IS IN ToWN. HE BROUGHT ME THIS HEART STUDDED COCK RING. I'M REALLY JUST OBLIGATED TO STAY HERE & HAVE SEX WITH HIM.

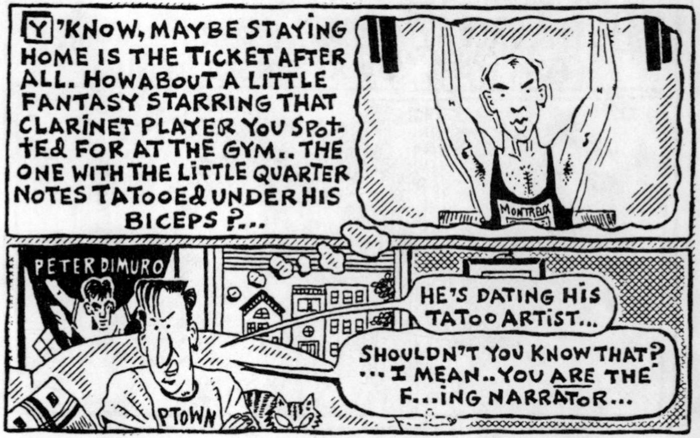
Y'KNOW, MAYBE STAYING HOME IS THE TICKET AFTER ALL. HOWABouT A LITTLE FANTASY STARRING THAT CLARINET PLAYER YOU SPOTTED FOR AT THE GYM.. THE ONE WITH THE LITTLE QUARTER NOTES TATOOED UNDER HIS BICEPS?...
MONTREUX
PETER DIMURO
PTOWN
HE'S DATING HIS TATOO ARTIST...
SHOULDN'T YOU KNOW THAT? ... I MEAN.. YOU ARE THE F...ING NARRATOR...

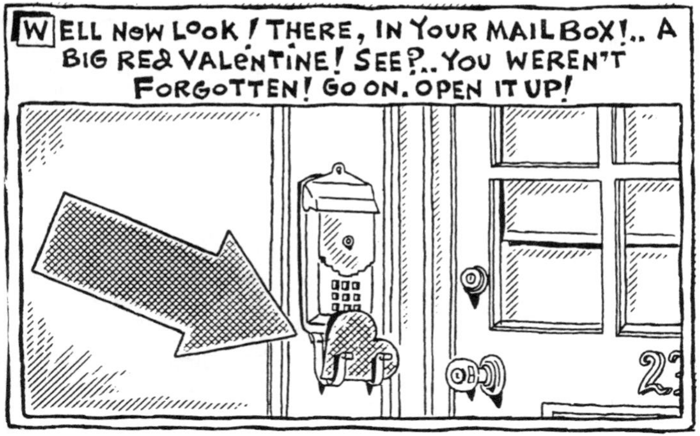
WELL NOW LOOK! THERE, IN YOUR MAILBOX!.. A BIG RED VALENTINE! SEE?.. YOU WEREN'T FORGOTTEN! GO ON. OPEN IT UP!
23

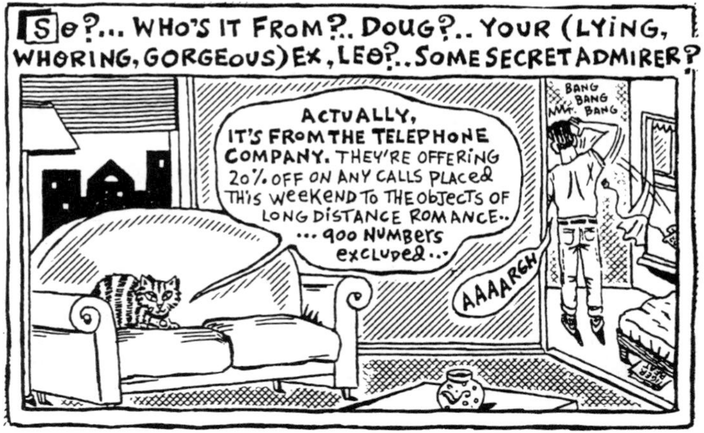
SO?... WHO'S IT FROM?.. DOUG?.. YOUR (LYING, WHORING, GORGEOUS) EX, LEO?.. SOME SECRET ADMIRER?
ACTUALLY, IT'S FROM THE TELEPHONE COMPANY. THEY'RE OFFERING 20% OFF ON ANY CALLS PLACED THIS WEEKEND TO THE OBJECTS OF LONG DISTANCE ROMANCE.. ...900 NUMBERS EXCLUDED...
BANG BANG BANG
AAAARGH

end.

Nothing to Wear...

So it's 9PM on a Saturday night. Your best friend Bucky just called to report (how he knows these things you'll never figure) that that clarinet player you think is sexy - the one with the tatoos - will probably be at Todd's party tonight..

YOW MYOWL MEYOW

LISTEN, I'M OPENING A CAN OF LENTIL SOUP - GOT THAT? S-O-U-P. HOW MANY YEARS'LL IT TAKE TO CONVINCE YOU THAT JUST CUZ YOU HEAR A CANOPENER - YOU'RE NOT GUARANTEED A CAN OF TUNA

MYOWL! ARE YOU HEARING ME? NO TUNA GUARANTEES

MYOWL OH FOR CHRISSAKES.

And although you think Todd is an ass, and have a nagging "bug" of some sort or another, you're not going to spend happily ever after with the clarinet player (or anyone else) by staying in with your kleenex watching Murder She Wrote. You start thinking about what to wear..

"OL' COMFY" LAST WASHED: SOMETIME DURING THE CARTER PRESIDENCY.

JELLY CANDINER WEDS ANNOUNCE ENGAGEMENT OF GLENDA TED HARNECD

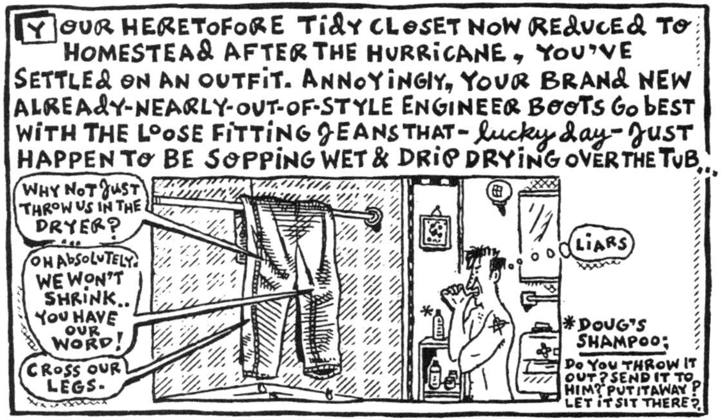
YOUR HERETOFORE TIDY CLOSET NOW REDUCED TO HOMESTEAD AFTER THE HURRICANE, YOU'VE SETTLED ON AN OUTFIT. ANNOYINGLY, YOUR BRAND NEW ALREADY-NEARLY-OUT-OF-STYLE ENGINEER BOOTS GO BEST WITH THE LOOSE FITTING JEANS THAT - lucky day - JUST HAPPEN TO BE SOPPING WET & DRIP DRYING OVER THE TUB...
WHY NOT JUST THROW US IN THE DRYER?
OH ABSOLUTELY. WE WON'T SHRINK.. YOU HAVE OUR WORD!
CROSS OUR LEGS.
LIARS
*DOUG'S SHAMPOO;
DO YOU THROW IT OUT? SEND IT TO HIM? PUT IT AWAY? LET IT SIT THERE?
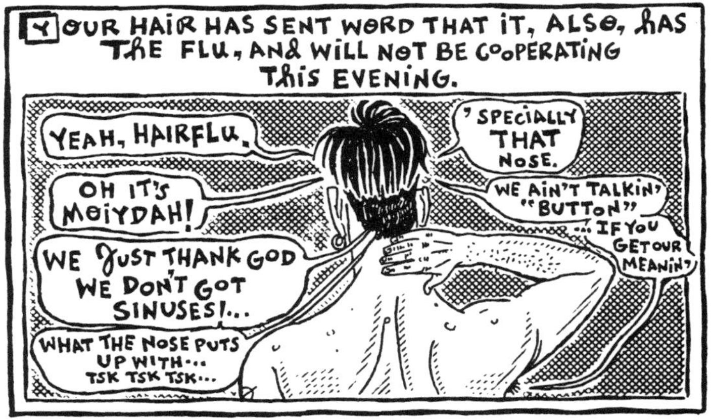
YOUR HAIR HAS SENT WORD THAT IT, ALSO, HAS THE FLU, AND WILL NOT BE COOPERATING THIS EVENING.
YEAH, HAIRFLU.
'SPECIALLY THAT NOSE.
OH IT'S MOIYDAH!
WE AIN'T TALKIN' "BUTTON" ... IF YOU GET OUR MEANIN'
WE JUST THANK GOD WE DON'T GOT SINUSES!...
WHAT THE NOSE PUTS UP WITH... TSK TSK TSK...

Continued...

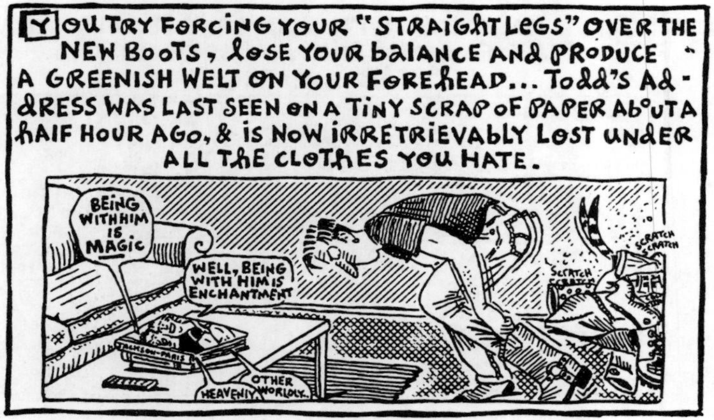
YOU TRY FORCING YOUR "STRAIGHT LEGS" OVER THE NEW BOOTS, LOSE YOUR BALANCE AND PRODUCE A GREENISH WELT ON YOUR FOREHEAD... TODD'S ADDRESS WAS LAST SEEN ON A TINY SCRAP OF PAPER ABOUT A HALF HOUR AGO, & IS NOW IRRETRIEVABLY LOST UNDER ALL THE CLOTHES YOU HATE.
BEING WITH HIM IS MAGIC
WELL, BEING WITH HIM IS ENCHANTMENT
HEAVENLY
OTHER WORLDLY..
SCRATCH SCRATCH
SCRATCH SCRATCH

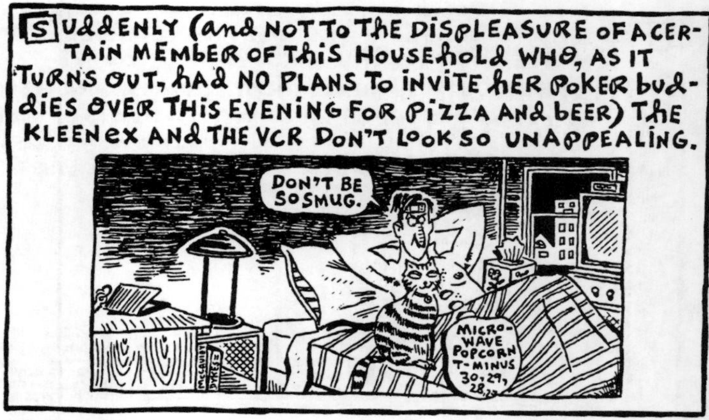
SUDDENLY (AND NOT TO THE DISPLEASURE OF A CERTAIN MEMBER OF THIS HOUSEHOLD WHO, AS IT TURNS OUT, HAD NO PLANS TO INVITE HER POKER BUDDIES OVER THIS EVENING FOR PIZZA AND BEER) THE KLEENEX AND THE VCR DON'T LOOK SO UNAPPEALING.
DON'T BE SO SMUG.
MICRO-WAVE POPCORN T-MINUS 30, 29, 28,

end.

PRIDE PART 1

PROUD SHE DIDN'T
THROW HERSELF OFF A BRIDGE AT AGE
19, WHEN SHE THOUGHT HER LESBIANISM
MEANT A LIFE OF CERTAIN GRIEF
AND LONELINESS.

PROUD his SEXUALITY,
ONCE A THREAT TO his OWN SENSE
OF VIRILITY, IS NOW INSTEAD, A SOURCE
OF IT.

Continued...

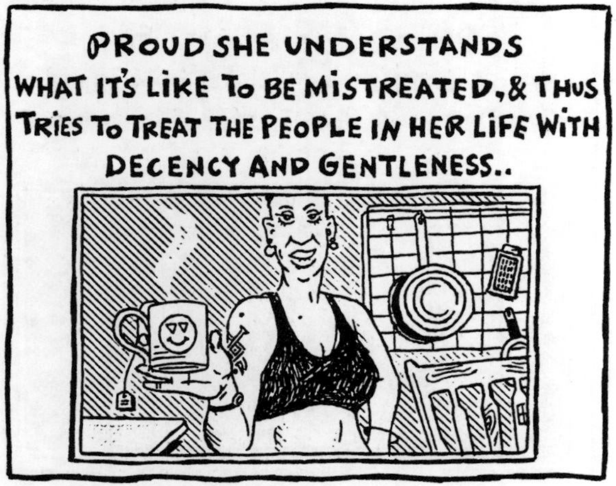
PROUD SHE UNDERSTANDS WHAT IT'S LIKE TO BE MISTREATED, & THUS TRIES TO TREAT THE PEOPLE IN HER LIFE WITH DECENCY AND GENTLENESS..

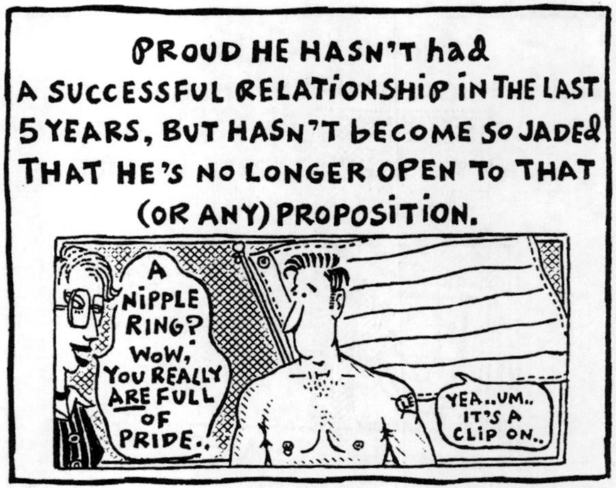
PROUD HE HASN'T had A SUCCESSFUL RELATIONSHIP IN THE LAST 5 YEARS, BUT HASN'T become SO JADED THAT HE'S NO LONGER OPEN TO THAT (OR ANY) PROPOSITION.
A NIPPLE RING? WOW, YOU REALLY ARE FULL OF PRIDE..
YEA..UM.. IT'S A CLIP ON..

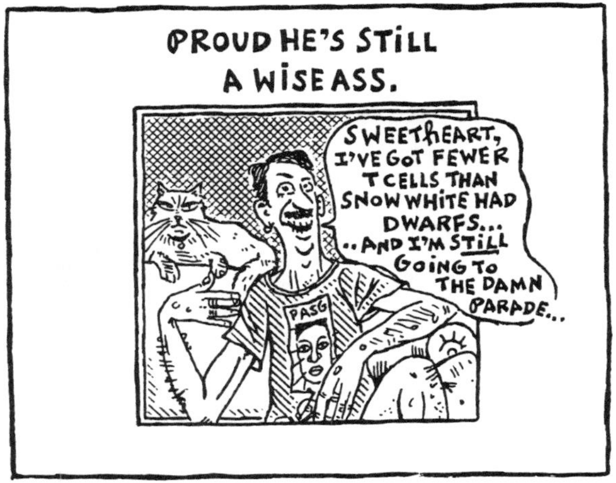
PROUD HE'S STILL A WISE ASS.
SWEETHEART, I'VE GOT FEWER T CELLS THAN SNOW WHITE HAD DWARFS... ..AND I'M STILL GOING TO THE DAMN PARADE...
PASG

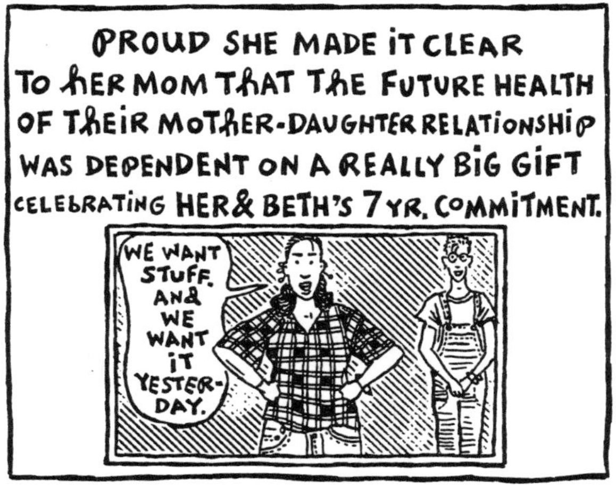
PROUD SHE MADE IT CLEAR TO HER MOM THAT THE FUTURE HEALTH OF THEIR MOTHER-DAUGHTER RELATIONSHIP WAS DEPENDENT ON A REALLY BIG GIFT CELEBRATING HER & BETH'S 7 YR. COMMITMENT.
WE WANT STUFF. AND WE WANT IT YESTER-DAY.

Continued...

PROUD THAT AS THE PARENT OF A GAY CHILD, SHE ROSE TO THE OCCASION.
LIZA & BETH HAPPY Anniversary

PROUD HE DOESN'T MIND WHO HE PISSES OFF.
DO US BOTH A FAVOR, SPEND A LITTLE LESS TIME FEELING MY PAIN, AND A LITTLE MORE TIME HONORING YOUR COMMITMENTS.

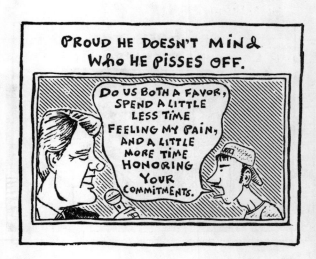

end.

WEEKENDING WITH ETIENNE

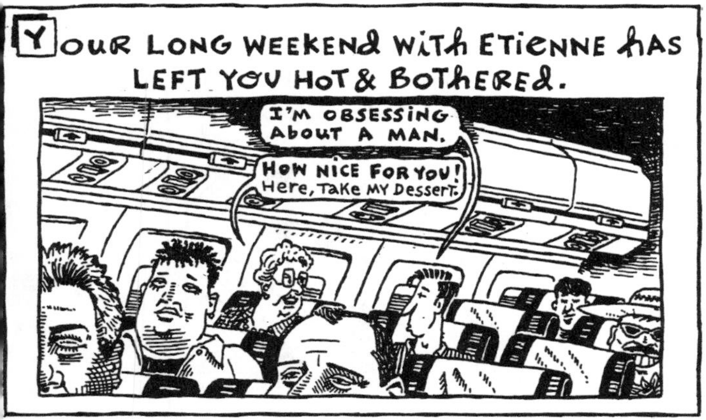
YOUR LONG WEEKEND WITH ETIENNE HAS LEFT YOU HOT & BOTHERED.
I'M OBSESSING ABOUT A MAN.
HOW NICE FOR YOU! Here, TAKE MY DESSERT.

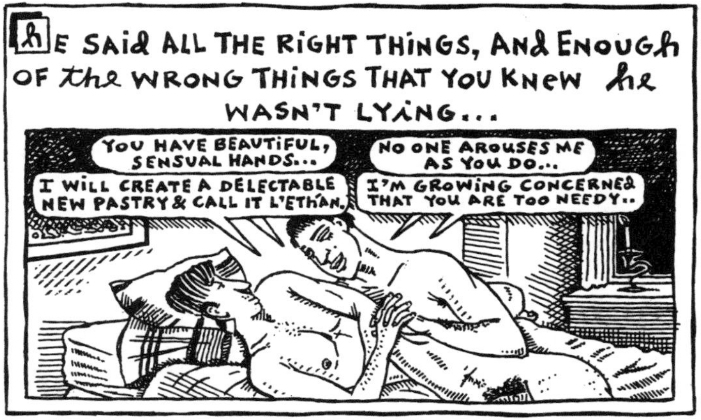
HE SAID ALL THE RIGHT THINGS, AND ENOUGH OF THE WRONG THINGS THAT YOU KNEW HE WASN'T LYING...
YOU HAVE BEAUTIFUL, SENSUAL HANDS...
I WILL CREATE A DELECTABLE NEW PASTRY & CALL IT L'ETHAN.
NO ONE AROUSES ME AS YOU DO...
I'M GROWING CONCERNED THAT YOU ARE TOO NEEDY..

Continued...

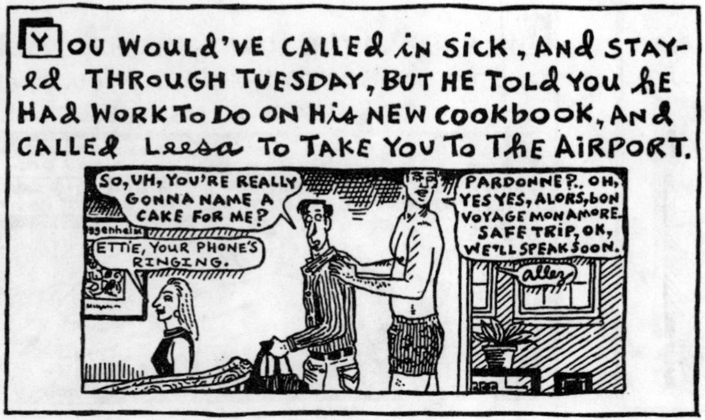
YOU WOULD'VE CALLED IN SICK, AND STAYED THROUGH TUESDAY, BUT HE TOLD YOU HE HAD WORK TO DO ON HIS NEW COOKBOOK, AND CALLED Leesa TO TAKE YOU TO THE AIRPORT.
SO, UH, YOU'RE REALLY GONNA NAME A CAKE FOR ME?
PARDONNE?.. OH, YES YES, ALORS, BON VOYAGE MON AMORE. SAFE TRIP, OK, WE'LL SPEAK SOON.
ETTIE, YOUR PHONE'S RINGING.
allez

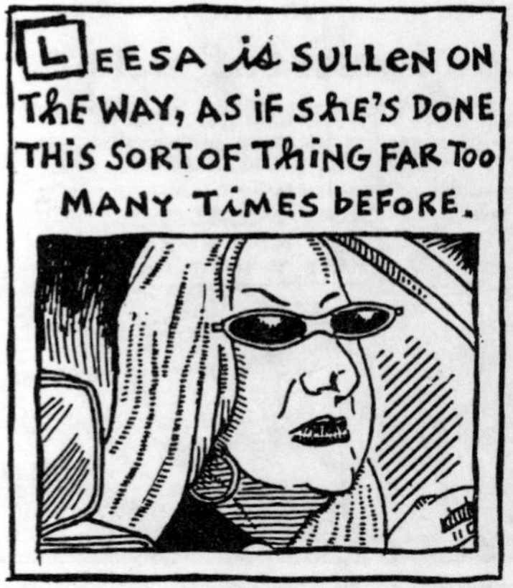
LEESA IS SULLEN ON THE WAY, AS IF SHE'S DONE THIS SORT OF THING FAR TOO MANY TIMES BEFORE.

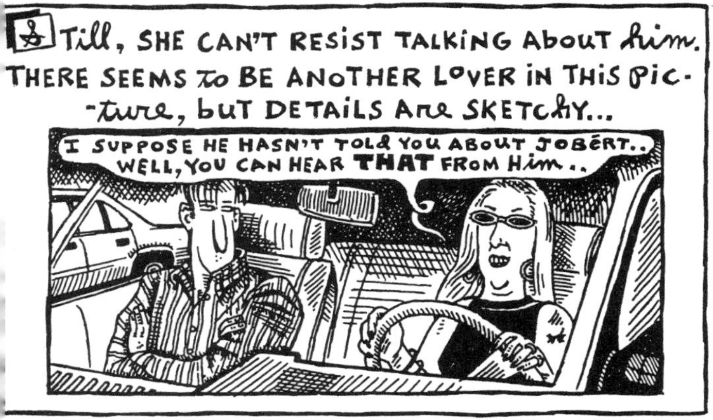
Still, SHE CAN'T RESIST TALKING ABOUT him. THERE SEEMS to BE ANOTHER LOVER IN THIS PIC-ture, but DETAILS ARE SKETCHY...
I SUPPOSE HE HASN'T TOLD YOU ABOUT JOBÉRT.. WELL, YOU CAN HEAR THAT FROM HIM..

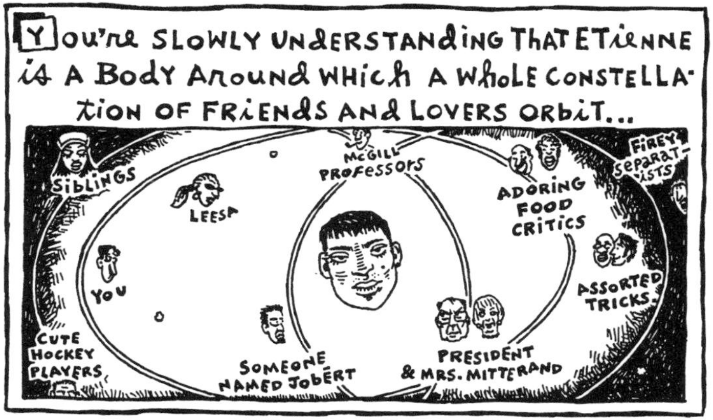
You're SLOWLY UNDERSTANDING THAT ETIENNE is A BODY AROUND WHICH A WHOLE CONSTELLA-TION OF FRIENDS AND LOVERS ORBIT...
SIBLINGS
LEESA
McGILL PROFESSORS
ADORING FOOD CRITICS
FIREY SEPARAT-ISTS
YOU
ASSORTED TRICKS
CUTE HOCKEY PLAYERS
SOMEONE NAMED JOBÉRT
PRESIDENT & MRS. MITTERAND

Continued...

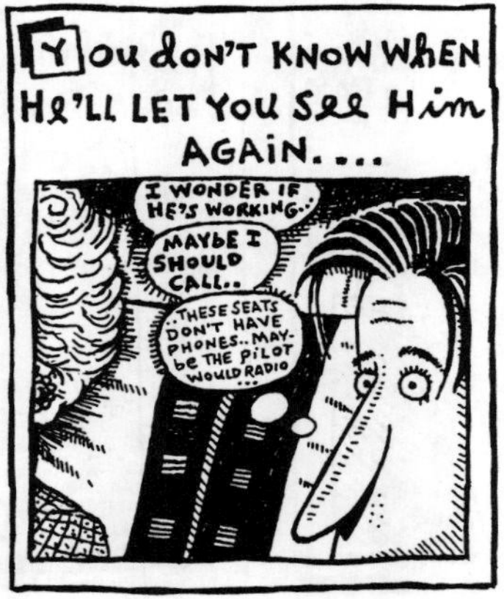
YOU DON'T KNOW WHEN HE'LL LET YOU SEE HIM AGAIN....
I WONDER IF HE'S WORKING..
MAYBE I SHOULD CALL..
..THESE SEATS DON'T HAVE PHONES.. MAYBE THE PILOT WOULD RADIO...

end.

MORE WEEKENDING WITH ETIENNE

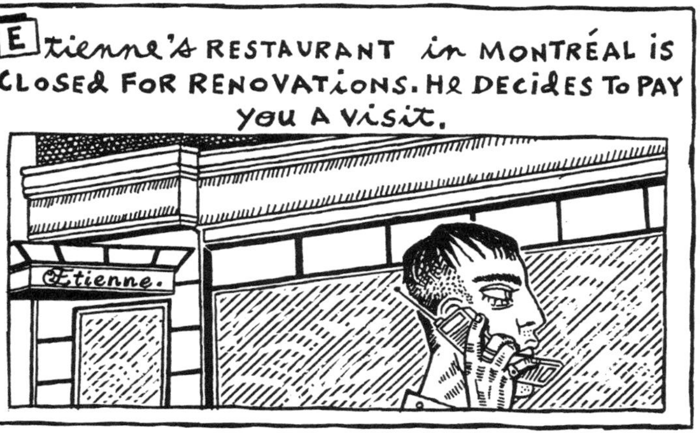
Etienne's RESTAURANT in MONTRÉAL IS CLOSED FOR RENOVATIONS. He DECIDES TO PAY you A visit.
Etienne.

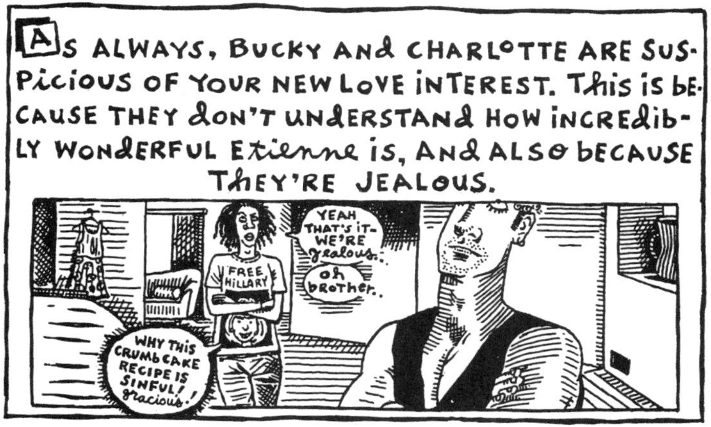
As ALWAYS, BUCKY AND CHARLOTTE ARE SUSPICIOUS OF YOUR NEW LOVE INTEREST. This is BECAUSE THEY DON'T UNDERSTAND HOW INCREDIBLY WONDERFUL Etienne IS, AND ALSO BECAUSE THEY'RE JEALOUS.
FREE HILLARY
WHY THIS CRUMBCAKE RECIPE IS SINFUL! gracious!
YEAH THAT'S IT- WE'RE jealous..
oh brother..

Continued...

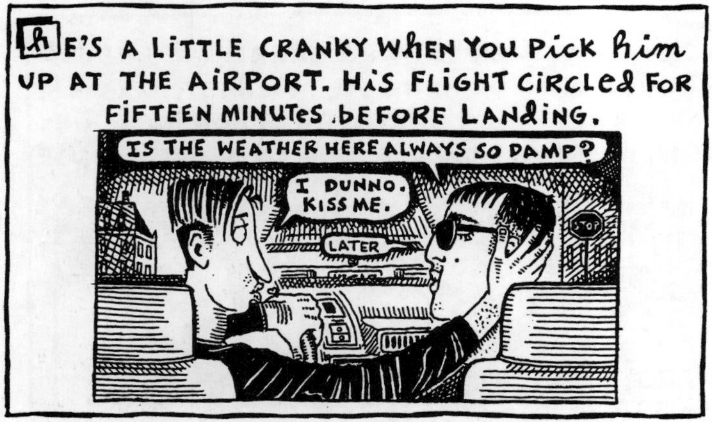
HE'S A LITTLE CRANKY WHEN YOU PICK HIM UP AT THE AIRPORT. HIS FLIGHT CIRCLED FOR FIFTEEN MINUTES BEFORE LANDING.
IS THE WEATHER HERE ALWAYS SO DAMP?
I DUNNO. KISS ME.
LATER
STOP

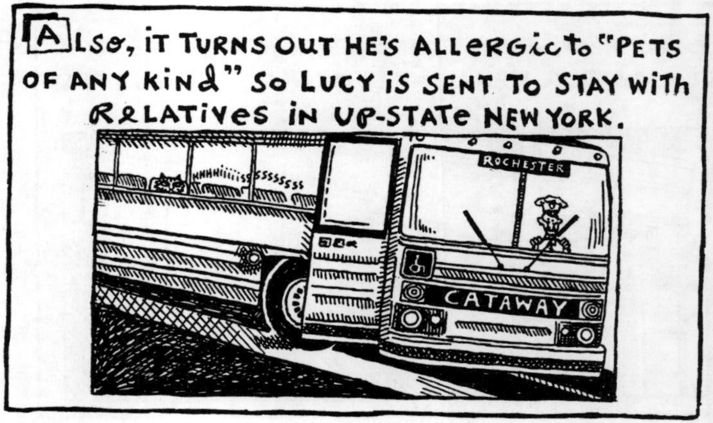
ALSO, IT TURNS OUT HE'S ALLERGIC TO "PETS OF ANY KIND" SO LUCY IS SENT TO STAY WITH RELATIVES IN UP-STATE NEW YORK.
ROCHESTER
CATAWAY

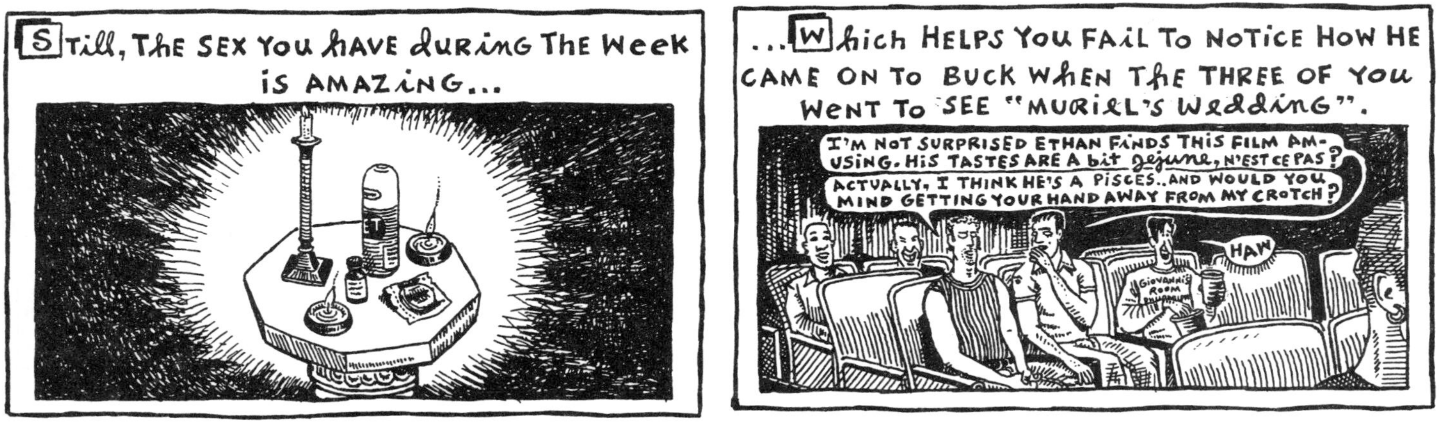
STILL, THE SEX YOU HAVE DURING THE WEEK IS AMAZING...
...WHICH HELPS YOU FAIL TO NOTICE HOW HE CAME ON TO BUCK WHEN THE THREE OF YOU WENT TO SEE "MURIEL'S WEDDING".
I'M NOT SURPRISED ETHAN FINDS THIS FILM AMUSING. HIS TASTES ARE A BIT *gejune*, N'EST CE PAS?
ACTUALLY, I THINK HE'S A PISCES.. AND WOULD YOU MIND GETTING YOUR HAND AWAY FROM MY CROTCH?
HAW
GIOVANNI'S ROOM

end.

PRIDE PART 2

It's late afternoon and another Pride celebration draws to a close...

So?.. Did'ja have fun?

Yeah.. I guess... The dancing was fun... and the parade was nice... I wish the guys on the manhole float wouldn't blow each other in front of the TV cameras... but... y'know.. other than that, it was ok, kinda like last year.

Yeah. These things seem to be coming up each year a little faster...

Yep.. (sigh).. so, Todd was pretty twisted.

She's always a mess at Pride.

Hey... why's that kid crying?

What kid?

Sniffle

PUSH BUT WA FO WA SIGN

BOXER '92

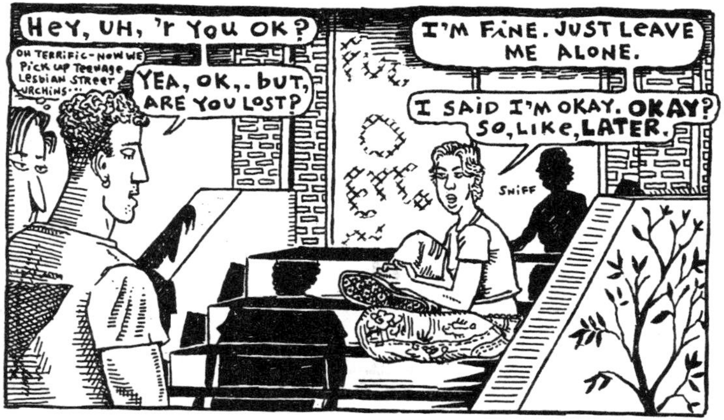
HEY, UH, 'R YOU OK?
OH TERRIFIC-NOW WE PICK UP TEENAGE LESBIAN STREET URCHINS...
YEA, OK,. BUT, ARE YOU LOST?
I'M FINE. JUST LEAVE ME ALONE.
I SAID I'M OKAY. OKAY? SO, LIKE, LATER.
SNIFF

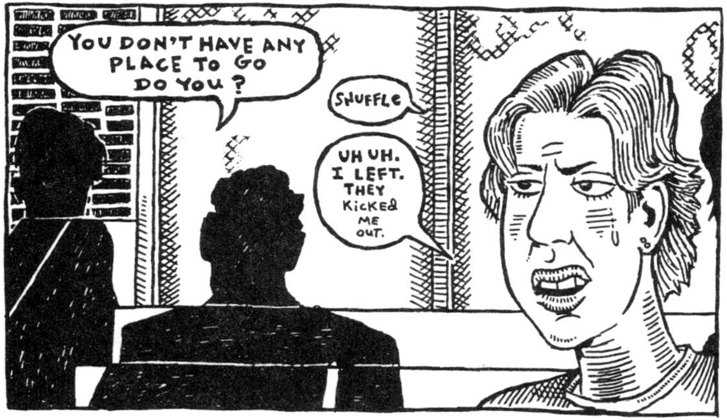
YOU DON'T HAVE ANY PLACE TO GO DO YOU?
SNUFFLE
UH UH. I LEFT. THEY KICKED ME OUT.

Continued...

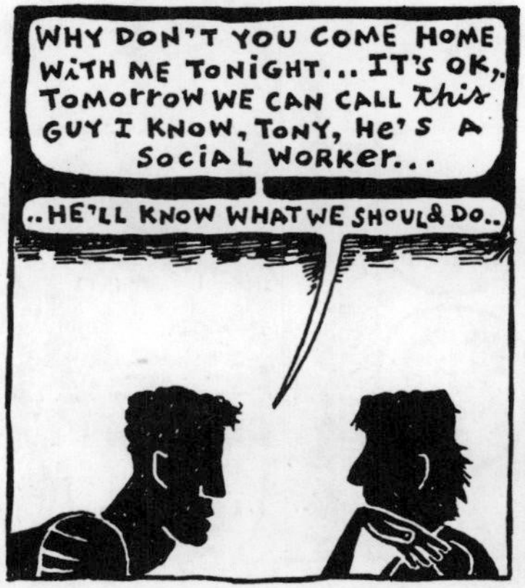
WHY DON'T YOU COME HOME WITH ME TONIGHT... IT'S OK,. TOMORROW WE CAN CALL this GUY I KNOW, TONY, HE'S A SOCIAL WORKER...
..HE'LL KNOW WHAT WE SHOULD DO..

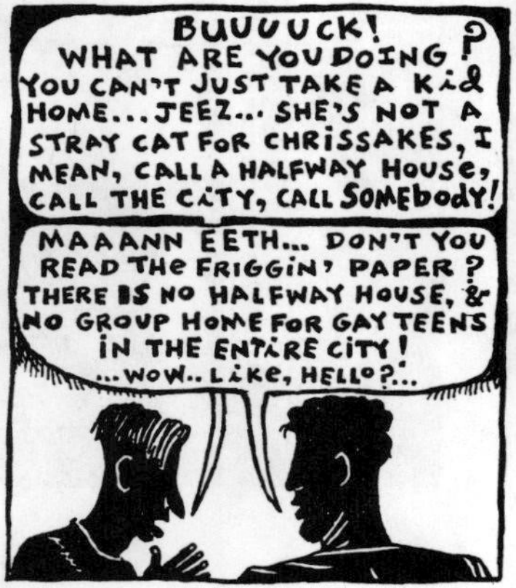
BUUUUCK! WHAT ARE YOU DOING? YOU CAN'T JUST TAKE A KID HOME...JEEZ... SHE'S NOT A STRAY CAT FOR CHRISSAKES, I MEAN, CALL A HALFWAY HOUSE, CALL THE CITY, CALL SOMEBODY!
MAAANN EETH... DON'T YOU READ THE FRIGGIN' PAPER? THERE IS NO HALFWAY HOUSE, & NO GROUP HOME FOR GAY TEENS IN THE ENTIRE CITY! ...WOW.. LIKE, HELLO?...

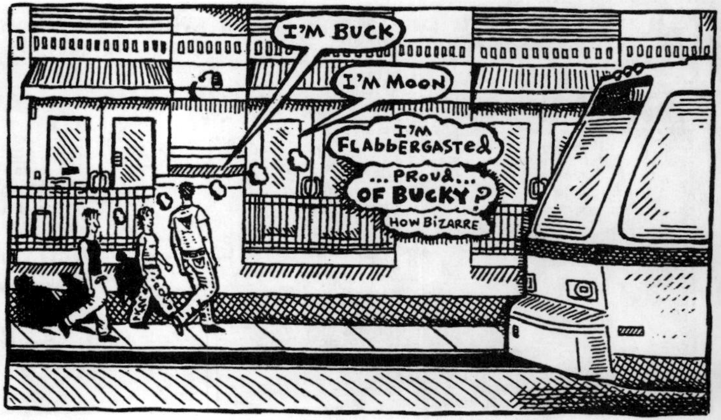
I'M BUCK
I'M MOON
I'M FLABBERGASTED
... PROUD... OF BUCKY?
HOW BIZARRE

end.

ETIENNE ENSCONCED.

YOUR FRIENDS MAY DOUBT ETIENNE'S SIN-
CERITY, BUT NOT THE BOEUF BOURGUIGNONNE
HE SERVED LAST NIGHT...

I DON'T USUALLY EAT MEAT, BUT I GOTTA SAY, THIS IS EXTRAORDINARY.

OH PLEASE

NO MORE EXTRA-ORDINARY THAN YOUR CHEEKBONES CHARLOTTE.

IT'S TRUE ETIENNE, THIS IS AWESOME.

OH I'M CAPABLE OF SERVING UP THINGS FAR MORE PLEASURABLE.

I'LL SAY!

GIGGLE.

Tipsy.

THE NEXT MORNING, WHILE CHARLOTTE HELPS
YOU WORK ON THE STILL DISASTROUS KITCHEN,
HE HOLES UP IN THE BEDROOM, ARGUING ON THE
PHONE, YOU THINK WITH JOBERT...

SO WHO'S JOBERT?

I DON'T REALLY KNOW.. HIS FRIEND LEESA MEN-TIONED HIM..

AN OLD LOVER, MAYBE... THO' COME TO THINK OF IT, I THINK HE CALLED HIS BROTHER JOBERT ALSO.

...UH HUH..

Continued...

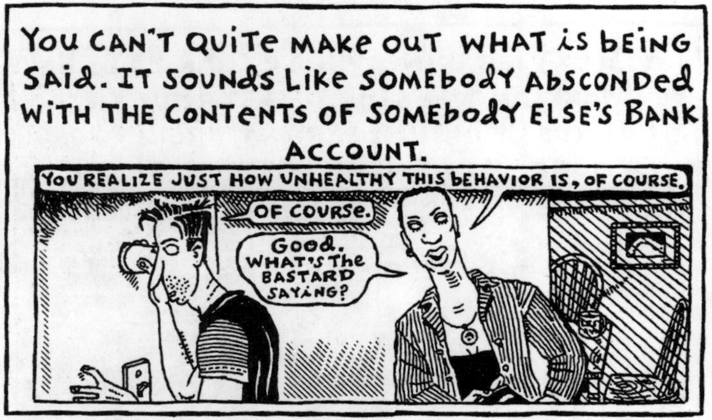
YOU CAN'T QUITE MAKE OUT WHAT IS BEING SAID. IT SOUNDS LIKE SOMEBODY ABSCONDED WITH THE CONTENTS OF SOMEBODY ELSE'S BANK ACCOUNT.
YOU REALIZE JUST HOW UNHEALTHY THIS BEHAVIOR IS, OF COURSE.
OF COURSE.
GOOD. WHAT'S THE BASTARD SAYING?

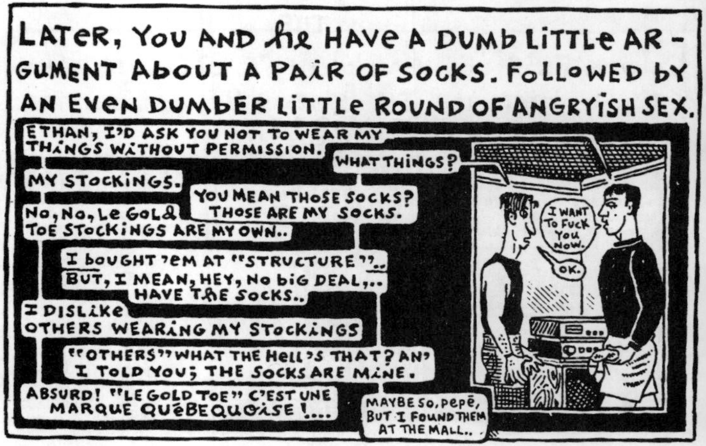
LATER, YOU AND HE HAVE A DUMB LITTLE ARGUMENT ABOUT A PAIR OF SOCKS. FOLLOWED BY AN EVEN DUMBER LITTLE ROUND OF ANGRYISH SEX.
ETHAN, I'D ASK YOU NOT TO WEAR MY THINGS WITHOUT PERMISSION.
WHAT THINGS?
MY STOCKINGS.
YOU MEAN THOSE SOCKS? THOSE ARE MY SOCKS.
NO, NO, LE GOLD TOE STOCKINGS ARE MY OWN..
I BOUGHT 'EM AT "STRUCTURE"..
BUT, I MEAN, HEY, NO BIG DEAL,.. HAVE THE SOCKS..
I DISLIKE OTHERS WEARING MY STOCKINGS
"OTHERS" WHAT THE HELL'S THAT? AN' I TOLD YOU; THE SOCKS ARE MINE.
ABSURD! "LE GOLD TOE" C'EST UNE MARQUE QUÉBEQUOISE!...
MAYBE SO, PEPÉ, BUT I FOUND THEM AT THE MALL..
I WANT TO FUCK YOU NOW.
OK.

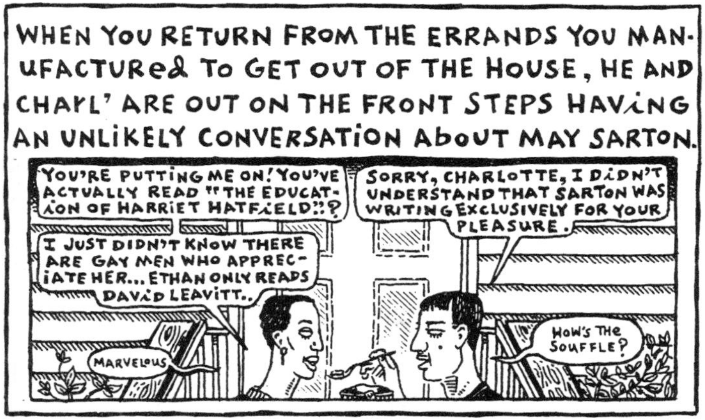
WHEN YOU RETURN FROM THE ERRANDS YOU MANUFACTURED TO GET OUT OF THE HOUSE, HE AND CHARL' ARE OUT ON THE FRONT STEPS HAVING AN UNLIKELY CONVERSATION ABOUT MAY SARTON.
YOU'RE PUTTING ME ON! YOU'VE ACTUALLY READ "THE EDUCATION OF HARRIET HATFIELD"!?
I JUST DIDN'T KNOW THERE ARE GAY MEN WHO APPRECIATE HER... ETHAN ONLY READS DAVID LEAVITT..
SORRY, CHARLOTTE, I DIDN'T UNDERSTAND THAT SARTON WAS WRITING EXCLUSIVELY FOR YOUR PLEASURE.
HOW'S THE SOUFFLE?
MARVELOUS

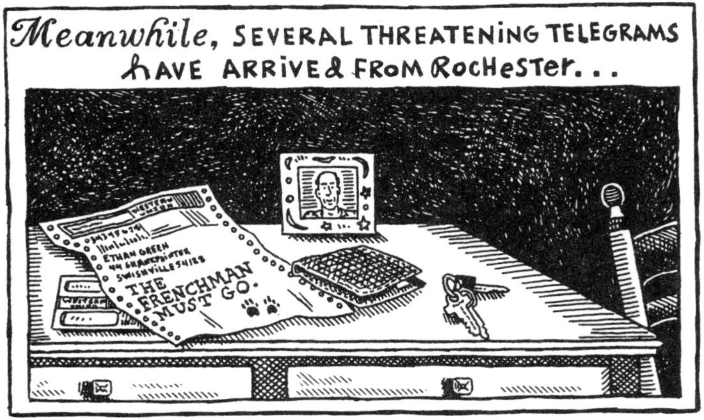
Meanwhile, SEVERAL THREATENING TELEGRAMS HAVE ARRIVED FROM ROCHESTER...
ETHAN GREEN
THE FRENCHMAN MUST GO.

end.

FATHERHOOD...

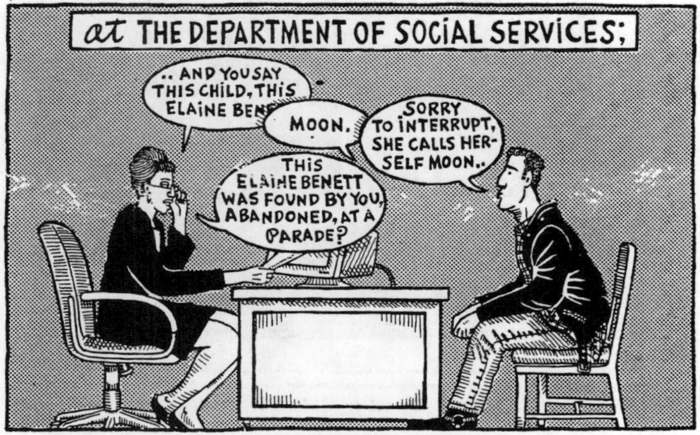
at THE DEPARTMENT OF SOCIAL SERVICES;
.. AND YOU SAY THIS CHILD, THIS ELAINE BEN
MOON.
SORRY TO INTERRUPT, SHE CALLS HER-SELF MOON..
THIS ELAINE BENETT WAS FOUND BY YOU, ABANDONED, AT A PARADE?

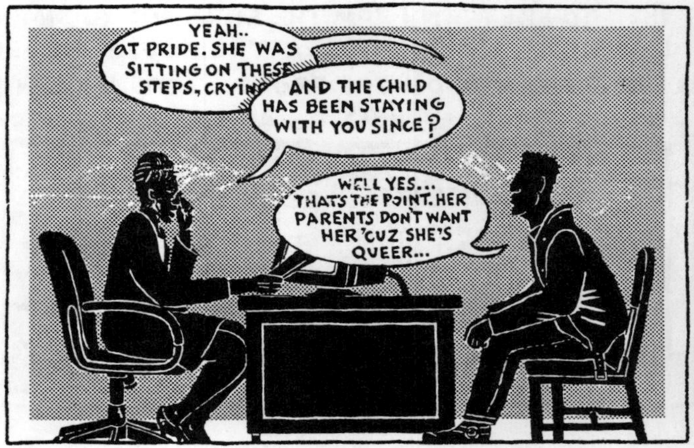
YEAH.. AT PRIDE. SHE WAS SITTING ON THESE STEPS, CRYIN
AND THE CHILD HAS BEEN STAYING WITH YOU SINCE?
WELL YES... THAT'S THE POINT. HER PARENTS DON'T WANT HER 'CUZ SHE'S QUEER...

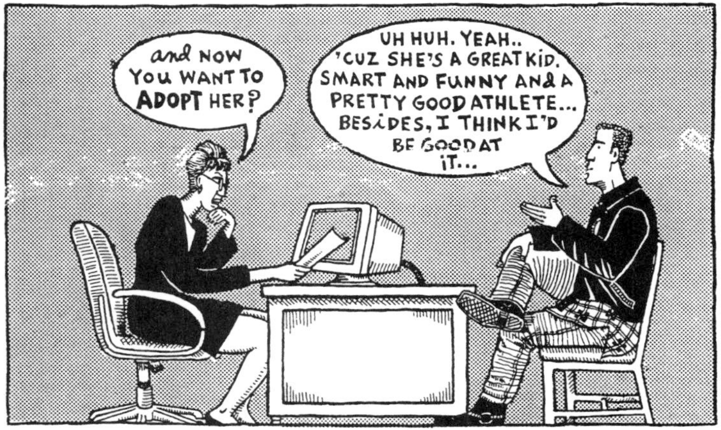
and NOW YOU WANT TO ADOPT HER?
UH HUH. YEAH.. 'CUZ SHE'S A GREAT KID. SMART AND FUNNY AND A PRETTY GOOD ATHLETE... BESIDES, I THINK I'D BE GOOD AT IT...

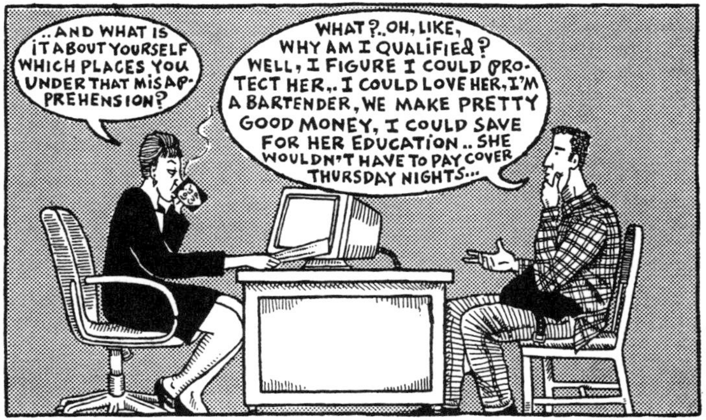
..AND WHAT IS IT ABOUT YOURSELF WHICH PLACES YOU UNDER THAT MISAPPREHENSION?
WHAT?..OH, LIKE, WHY AM I QUALIFIED? WELL, I FIGURE I COULD PROTECT HER,. I COULD LOVE HER, I'M A BARTENDER, WE MAKE PRETTY GOOD MONEY, I COULD SAVE FOR HER EDUCATION.. SHE WOULDN'T HAVE TO PAY COVER THURSDAY NIGHTS...

Continued...

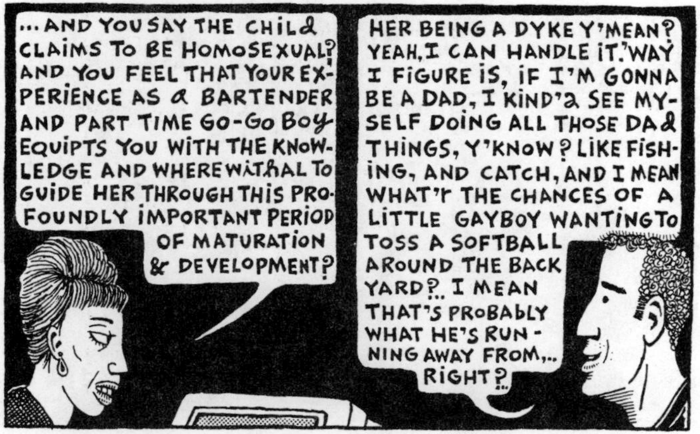
...AND YOU SAY THE CHILD CLAIMS TO BE HOMOSEXUAL? AND YOU FEEL THAT YOUR EXPERIENCE AS A BARTENDER AND PART TIME GO-GO BOY EQUIPTS YOU WITH THE KNOWLEDGE AND WHEREWITHAL TO GUIDE HER THROUGH THIS PROFOUNDLY IMPORTANT PERIOD OF MATURATION & DEVELOPMENT?
HER BEING A DYKE Y'MEAN? YEAH, I CAN HANDLE IT. WAY I FIGURE IS, IF I'M GONNA BE A DAD, I KIND'A SEE MYSELF DOING ALL THOSE DAD THINGS, Y'KNOW? LIKE FISHING, AND CATCH, AND I MEAN WHAT'R THE CHANCES OF A LITTLE GAYBOY WANTING TO TOSS A SOFTBALL AROUND THE BACK YARD?.. I MEAN THAT'S PROBABLY WHAT HE'S RUNNING AWAY FROM,.. RIGHT?..

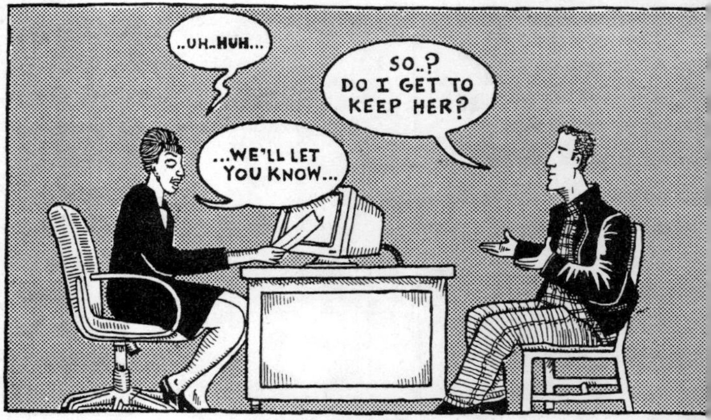
SO..? DO I GET TO KEEP HER?
..UH..HUH...
...WE'LL LET YOU KNOW...

end

KITCHEN RAP...

HEY?
ANYONE HOME?
EETH?
ETHAN?
IN HERE...
WHATSUP ?...OH JESUS.. ARE YOU STILL WRITING THAT LETTER TO THE EDITOR?
YEA, SO? HI MOON...IT PISSES ME OFF. ALL THE PAIN IN THIS WORLD AND YET, THE ONLY THING THIS ASS HAS TO BRAY ABOUT IS TOO MUCH FETTISH FLAUNTING AT THE PRIDE PARADE.

Continued...

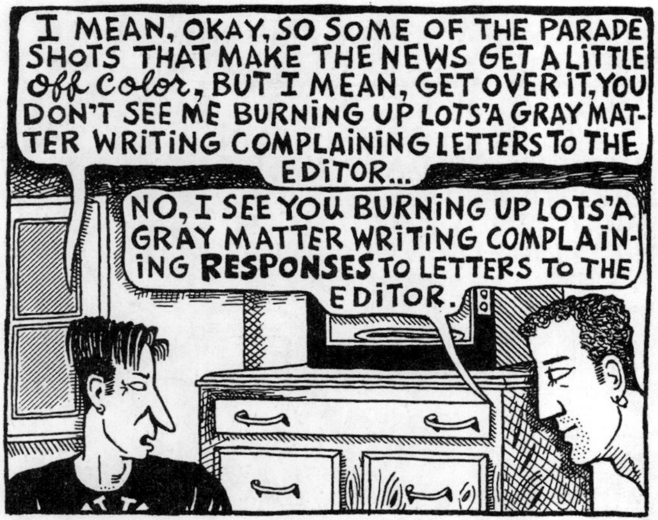
I MEAN, OKAY, SO SOME OF THE PARADE SHOTS THAT MAKE THE NEWS GET A LITTLE *off color*, BUT I MEAN, GET OVER IT, YOU DON'T SEE ME BURNING UP LOTS'A GRAY MATTER WRITING COMPLAINING LETTERS TO THE EDITOR...
NO, I SEE YOU BURNING UP LOTS'A GRAY MATTER WRITING COMPLAINING **RESPONSES** TO LETTERS TO THE EDITOR.

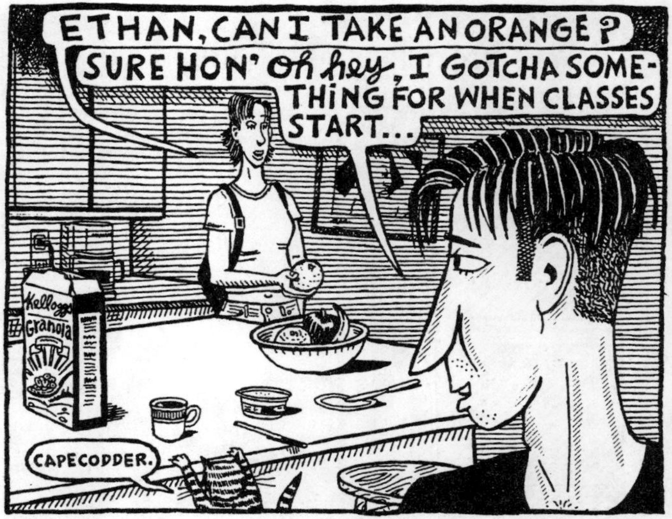
ETHAN, CAN I TAKE AN ORANGE?
SURE HON' *oh hey*, I GOTCHA SOMETHING FOR WHEN CLASSES START...
Kellogg's Granola
CAPECODDER.

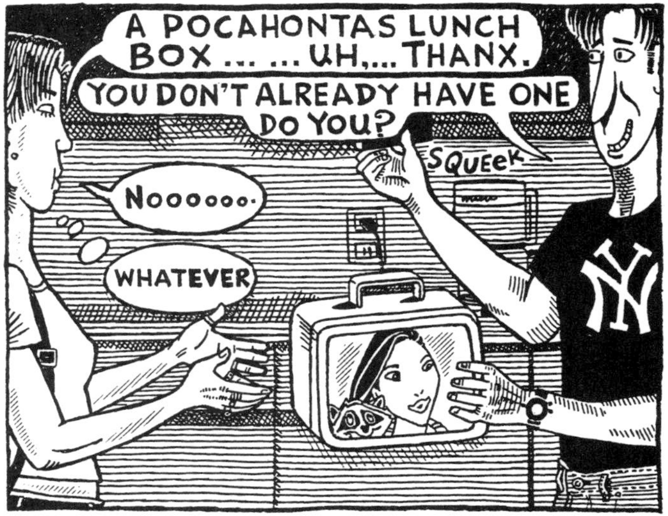
A POCAHONTAS LUNCH BOX ... ... UH,... THANX.
YOU DON'T ALREADY HAVE ONE DO YOU?
SQUEEK
Nooooooo.
WHATEVER

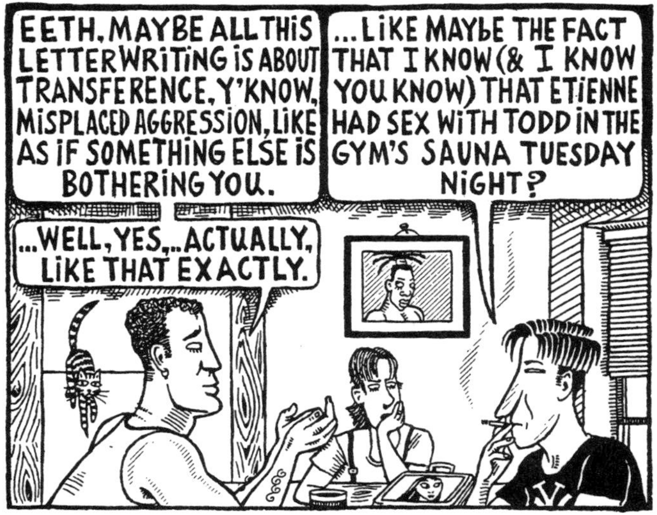
EETH, MAYBE ALL THIS LETTER WRITING IS ABOUT TRANSFERENCE, Y'KNOW, MISPLACED AGGRESSION, LIKE AS IF SOMETHING ELSE IS BOTHERING YOU.
...LIKE MAYBE THE FACT THAT I KNOW (& I KNOW YOU KNOW) THAT ETIENNE HAD SEX WITH TODD IN THE GYM'S SAUNA TUESDAY NIGHT?
...WELL, YES,..ACTUALLY, LIKE THAT EXACTLY.

Continued...

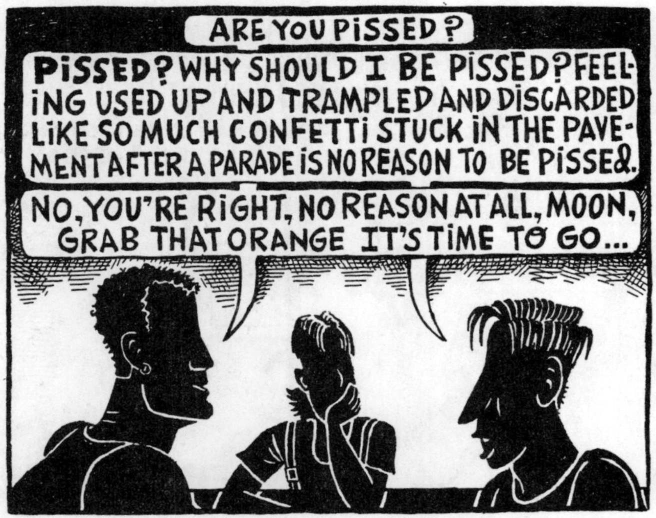
ARE YOU PISSED?
PISSED? WHY SHOULD I BE PISSED? FEELING USED UP AND TRAMPLED AND DISCARDED LIKE SO MUCH CONFETTI STUCK IN THE PAVEMENT AFTER A PARADE IS NO REASON TO BE PISSED.
NO, YOU'RE RIGHT, NO REASON AT ALL, MOON, GRAB THAT ORANGE IT'S TIME TO GO...

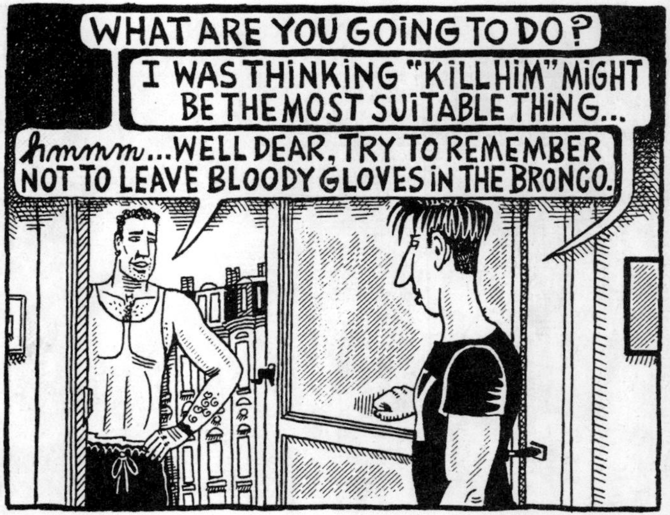
WHAT ARE YOU GOING TO DO?
I WAS THINKING "KILL HIM" MIGHT BE THE MOST SUITABLE THING...
hmmm... WELL DEAR, TRY TO REMEMBER NOT TO LEAVE BLOODY GLOVES IN THE BRONCO.

end.

THE
ETHAN GREEN
CONTRACT WITH
AMERICA

AS MUCH THERAPY AS YOU CAN STAND.
(NO COPAYMENT)
... SO ANYWAY, AS I WAS SAYING, ETIENNE IS LIKE THIS COMPLETE ASS. BUT HE'S CERTAINLY GOT A CUTE ASS, HA HA! I MEAN IT'S LIKE I HAVEN'T BEEN SO TURNED ON IN YEARS!.. 'CAUSE.. WELL.. THIS'S A LITTLE EMBARRASSING, I MEAN, HE LIKES IT A BIT.. (EHEM).. ROUGH, Y'KNOW.. WELL, DOUG ACTUALLY DID LIKE THAT TOO, SOMETIMES.. BUT I LOVED DOUG, Y'KNOW? SO THAT'S KIND OF DIFFERENT PROBABLY... I GUESS...
SAY, THIS UNLIMITED THERAPY DEAL'S PRETTY FABULOUS!
GOOD THING I THUNK IT UP..
PALM READINGS
FAG DRAMA

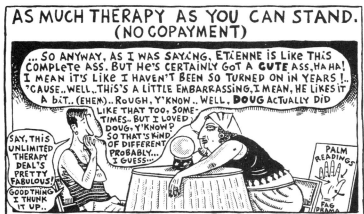

Continued...

TIGHTER "ABS" (MORE GERMAN CHOCOLATE CAKE) TASK FORCE.
HEY, SHOULDN'T WE BE DOING S'MORE "CRUNCHES"?.... I MEAN, IT DOES SAY "TIGHTER ABS" (MORE GERMAN CHOCOLATE CAKE) TASK FORCE.
BELCH
RUMBLE
LOOK, YOU WANNA BE A BOYSCOUT? DO IT ON YER OWN TIME. NOT UNCLE SAM'S. NOW SHADDUPH AN' EAT MORE OF THAT CAKE...
GROAN
THREE PAID DAYS OFF BEFORE HALLOWEEN TO PLAN COSTUME.
THIS IS AN ESPECIALLY IMPORTANT ASPECT OF OUR PROPOSAL.
HALLOWEEN MUST BE HONORED!
IN DENMARK THEY GET 5 DAYS OFF FOR THIS, Y'KNOW.
OH IT'S TRUE!

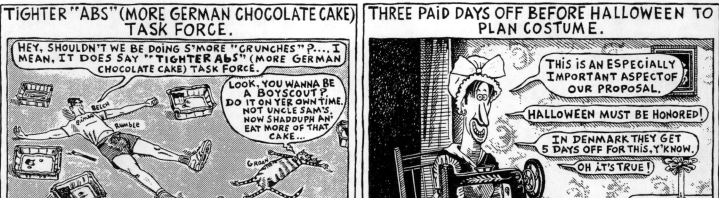

NO SALES TAX ON CUTE OUTFITS.

MR. SPEAKER, OBVIOUSLY THIS BILL'S NECESSITY IS LOST ON YOU, BECAUSE SIR, YOU **HAVE NO** CUTE OUTFITS. HOWEVER FOR MILLIONS OF STYLISH GAY MEN, & THEIR LIPSTICK LESBIAN ALLIES, THE PURCHASE OF VERSACE, DIESEL & GAUTIER IS A MATTER OF GRAVE CONSEQUENCE.

LOBSTER NEWBERG SCHOOL LUNCH INITIATIVE.

BUT, ETHAN, IF CATSUP ISN'T THE VEGETABLE ANYMORE, WHAT IS?

EXPENSIVE CARROT CAKE.

GOODY!

BUFF NEW GUY AT THE GYM WILL BE HOT FOR YOU, WON'T NOTICE YOUR BEST FRIEND AT ALL, PILOT PROGRAM.

OH YEA.

OH MY.

OH Please

end.

Summer House Diary
with ethanGreen

10:30 am
WAKE UP. BYPASS THE COMMUNAL "CHOCK FULL O' NUTS" FOR A FULL POT OF A *housemate's* PRIVATE STASH OF KONA...

MUST HAVE THE COFFEE MUST HAVE THE COFFEE

HEHHEHHEH

11:15 am
DECIDE TO WORK OUT BEFORE YOU GO TO THE BEACH. THEN UNDECIDE. THEN DECIDE AGAIN. REALIZE THAT AS YOU'VE BEEN DECIDING, A HOUSEMATE'S IDIOT WESTIE HAS EATEN YOUR WEIGHT LIFTING GLOVES...

11:30 am

GRILL ANOTHER HOUSEMATE'S TRICK AS HE'S COLLECTING HIS THINGS TO LEAVE...

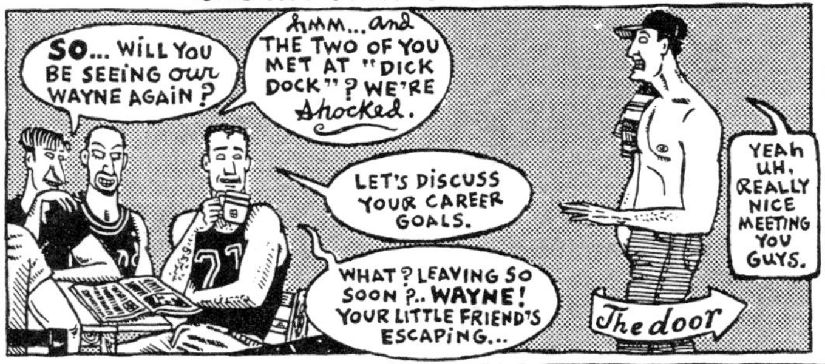
SO... WILL YOU BE SEEING *our* WAYNE AGAIN?
hmm...and THE TWO OF YOU MET AT "DICK DOCK"? WE'RE *shocked*.
LET'S DISCUSS YOUR CAREER GOALS.
WHAT? LEAVING SO SOON?.. WAYNE! YOUR LITTLE FRIEND'S ESCAPING...
YEAH UH, REALLY NICE MEETING YOU GUYS.
The door

9:15pm

DEMAND A HOUSEMEETING BECAUSE NO ONE EVER EMPTIES THE DISHWASHER.

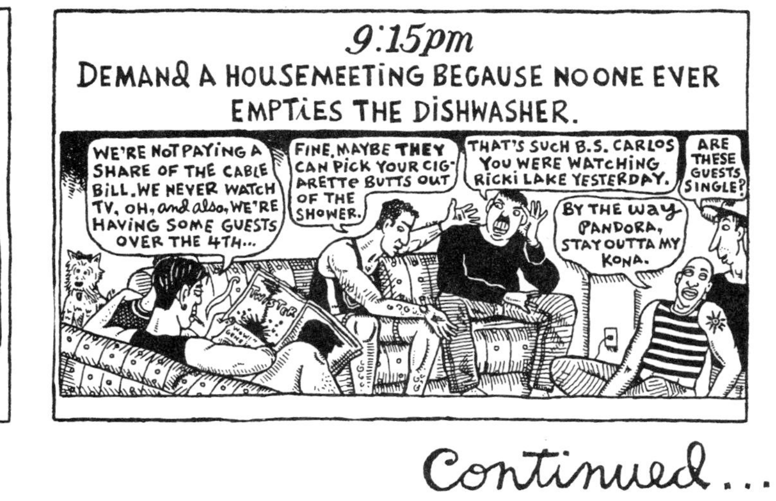
WE'RE NOT PAYING A SHARE OF THE CABLE BILL. WE NEVER WATCH TV, OH, *and also*, WE'RE HAVING SOME GUESTS OVER THE 4TH...
FINE, MAYBE THEY CAN PICK YOUR CIGARETTE BUTTS OUT OF THE SHOWER.
THAT'S SUCH B.S. CARLOS YOU WERE WATCHING RICKI LAKE YESTERDAY.
ARE THESE GUESTS SINGLE?
BY THE *way* PANDORA, STAY OUTTA MY KONA.
TWISTER

Continued...

10:45pm
SLYLY PRESS "REDIAL" THE SECOND A HOUSEMATE HANGS UP THE PHONE, TO DISCOVER WHO SHE'S BEEN CALLING...
10:46pm
WISH YOU WEREN'T SO SLY..
HELLO.. HELLO? HELLO? OKAY, WELL I HEAR HEAVY BREATHING SO CUT THE SHIT CARLOS, WHEN'R YOU & YOUR HUNKY HUSBAND TIM HEADED OVER HERE? I'M LIKE A CAT IN HEAT I'M SO HORNY.. CARLOS? CARLOS?..
THAT'S JASON CHANG!

end.

THE LUV SPONGE.

ONE SATURDAY AFTERNOON WHEN YOU SHOULD'VE BEEN SCRUBBING THE BATHROOM, YOU AND A CELEBRATED TELEVISION PITCHMAN FELL DEEPLY IN LOVE.
MC
ZSTZSZZ
HE WORKED A GREAT DEAL. YOU SPENT MOST OF YOUR TIME BY HIS POOL.
BACK AT SIX LUV SPONGE.
RING

Continued...

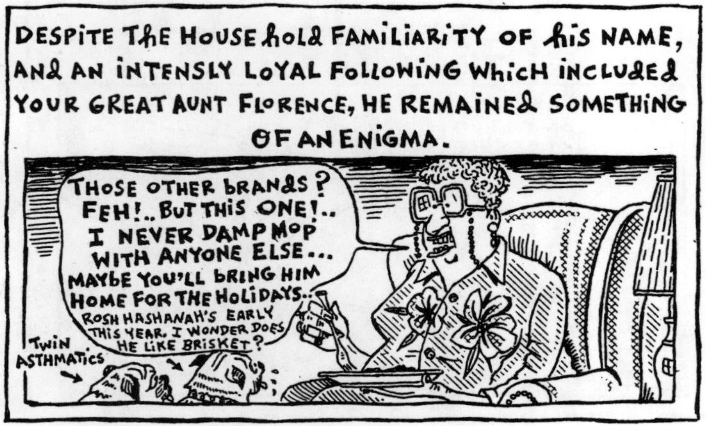
DESPITE THE HOUSEHOLD FAMILIARITY OF HIS NAME, AND AN INTENSLY LOYAL FOLLOWING WHICH INCLUDED YOUR GREAT AUNT FLORENCE, HE REMAINED SOMETHING OF AN ENIGMA.
THOSE OTHER BRANDS? FEH!.. BUT THIS ONE!.. I NEVER DAMP MOP WITH ANYONE ELSE... MAYBE YOU'LL BRING HIM HOME FOR THE HOLIDAYS.. ROSH HASHANAH'S EARLY THIS YEAR. I WONDER DOES HE LIKE BRISKET?
TWIN ASTHMATICS

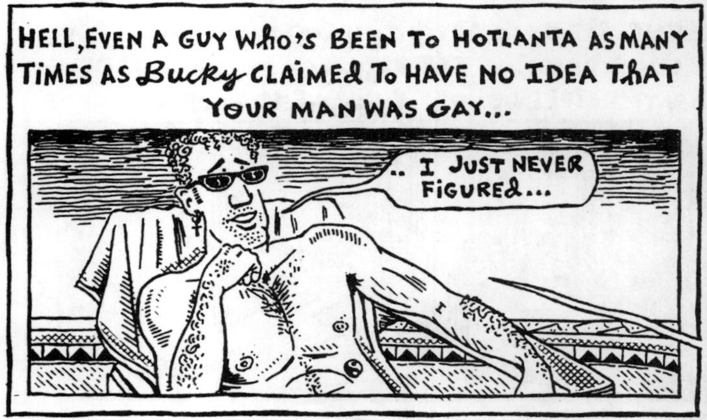
HELL, EVEN A GUY WHO'S BEEN TO HOTLANTA AS MANY TIMES AS *Bucky* CLAIMED TO HAVE NO IDEA THAT YOUR MAN WAS GAY...
.. I JUST NEVER FIGURED...

'COURSE BUCK ISN'T THE BRIGHTEST bulb BURNING, AND PROBABLY FELT A BIT SILLY WHEN YOU POINTED OUT A FEW SALIENT POINTS...

..HE'S GOT A GREAT TAN, ROLLED UP SLEEVES WHICH SHOW OFF SWELLING BICEPS, EARRINGS, AND AN OBSESSION WITH CLEANING HOUSE... WHAT DO YOU THINK?!!

GOSH, YOU'RE RIGHT..

I DUNNO. I MEAN, THE GUY DOES WEAR WHITE SLACKS BEFORE MEMORIAL DAY.

TRUE, he liked HIS SEX KIND'a STERILE, BUT YOU FIGURED TIME AND A LITTLE bit OF ELBOW GREASE WOULD REMEDY THAT...

I'M HOME!

WASH ME BABY, I FEEL dirty.

WAY dirty.

end.

GUNTHER'S ILLNESS...

YOU KNEW GUNTHER FROM WHEN YOU WERE WITH DOUG. THEY BECAME FRIENDS-OR FUCKBUDDIES-BACK WHEN DOUG WAS FIRST COMING OUT & GOING TO THE BARS.

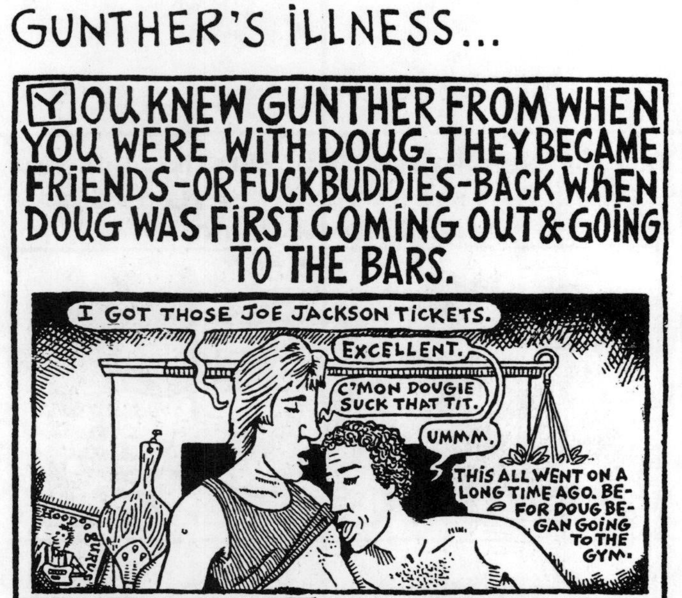
I GOT THOSE JOE JACKSON TICKETS.
EXCELLENT.
C'MON DOUGIE SUCK THAT TIT.
UMMM.
THIS ALL WENT ON A LONG TIME AGO. BEFOR DOUG BEGAN GOING TO THE GYM.
HOODOO GURUS

LAST SPRING GUNTHER GOT SICK. PAUL, HIS LOVER, BEGAN TURNING TO DOUG FOR HELP; RUNNING ERRANDS, AND STAYING WITH GUNTHER WHEN PAUL HAD TO WORK.

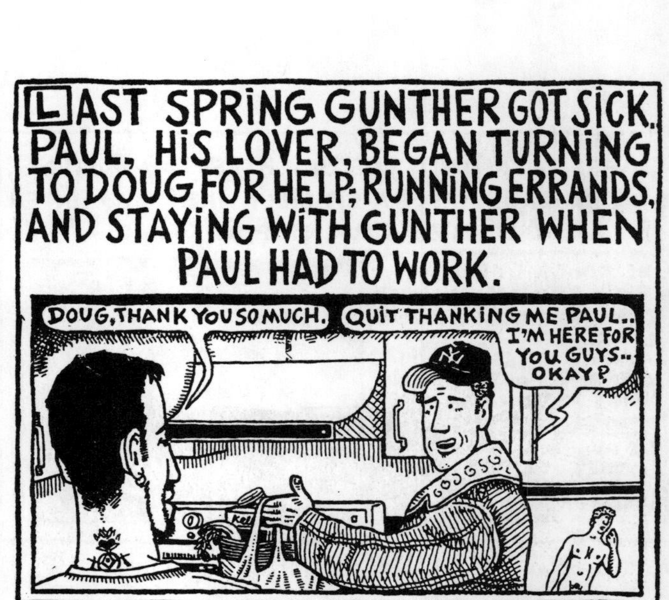
DOUG, THANK YOU SO MUCH.
QUIT THANKING ME PAUL.. I'M HERE FOR YOU GUYS... OKAY?

DOUG BEGAN RELYING MORE ON YOU. YOU'D ALWAYS LIKED GUNTHER & PAUL, AND BEING ASKED TO HELP MADE YOU FEEL INCLUDED. PART OF SOMETHING.

DOUG IT'S NO TROUBLE. REALLY I'D LIKE TO.. OK, I'LL SEE YOU AT FOUR...

PEANUT

HATCHING SOME PLOT TO MAKE OFF WITH ENTIRE JAR.

GUNTHER DIDN'T TAKE ANY SHIT. WHEN CYBELLE, A HOME-CARE PROVIDER, OBJECTED THAT HIS FAVORITE CANDLES MIGHT DETONATE HIS PORTABLE OXYGEN TANK, HE FIRED HER.

OK, I AM SO OUT OF HERE..

SWEETIE, YOU WERE SO NEVER HERE IN THE FIRST PLACE.

WINCE

Continued...

LATER, HE INSISTED THAT PAUL & DOUG BURN SAGE IN THE BEDROOM. THIS, HE CLAIMED, WOULD CLEANSE THE SPACE OF ANY LINGERING, BUREAUCRATIC, HEALTH-CARE-INDUSTRY ENERGY.

LIKE THIS?

YEAH.

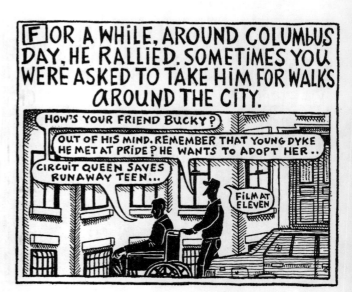

FOR A WHILE, AROUND COLUMBUS DAY, HE RALLIED. SOMETIMES YOU WERE ASKED TO TAKE HIM FOR WALKS AROUND THE CITY.

HOW'S YOUR FRIEND BUCKY?

OUT OF HIS MIND. REMEMBER THAT YOUNG DYKE HE MET AT PRIDE? HE WANTS TO ADOPT HER..

CIRCUIT QUEEN SAVES RUNAWAY TEEN...

FILM AT ELEVEN

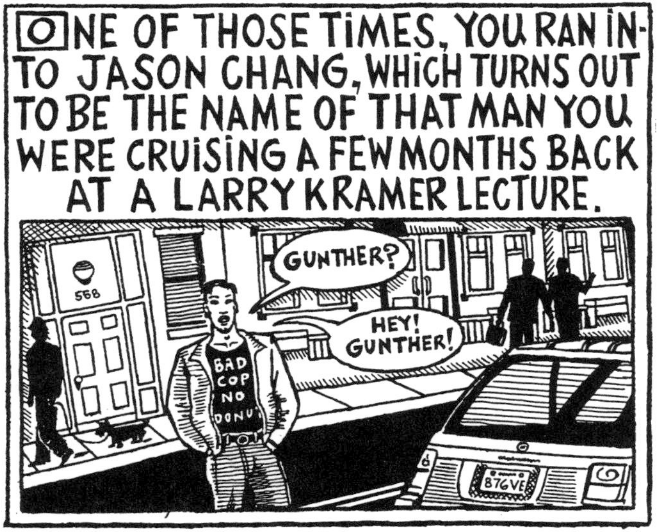
ONE OF THOSE TIMES, YOU RAN INTO JASON CHANG, WHICH TURNS OUT TO BE THE NAME OF THAT MAN YOU WERE CRUISING A FEW MONTHS BACK AT A LARRY KRAMER LECTURE.
558
GUNTHER?
HEY! GUNTHER!
BAD COP NO DONU
B76VE

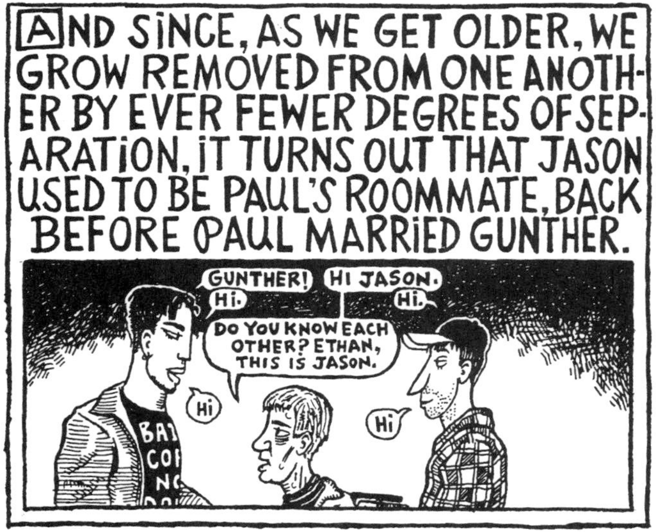
AND SINCE, AS WE GET OLDER, WE GROW REMOVED FROM ONE ANOTHER BY EVER FEWER DEGREES OF SEPARATION, IT TURNS OUT THAT JASON USED TO BE PAUL'S ROOMMATE, BACK BEFORE PAUL MARRIED GUNTHER.
GUNTHER!
Hi.
HI JASON.
Hi.
DO YOU KNOW EACH OTHER? ETHAN, THIS IS JASON.
Hi
Hi

end.

OVER & OUT.

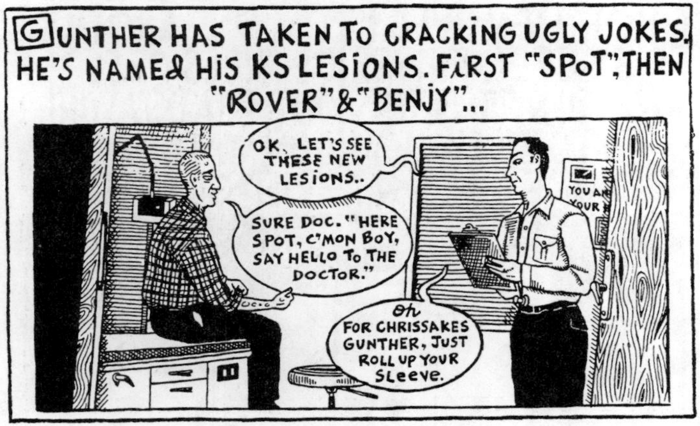
GUNTHER HAS TAKEN TO CRACKING UGLY JOKES. HE'S NAMED HIS KS LESIONS. FIRST "SPOT", THEN "ROVER" & "BENJY"...
OK, LET'S SEE THESE NEW LESIONS..
SURE DOC. "HERE SPOT, C'MON BOY, SAY HELLO TO THE DOCTOR."
Oh FOR CHRISSAKES GUNTHER, JUST ROLL UP YOUR SLEEVE.

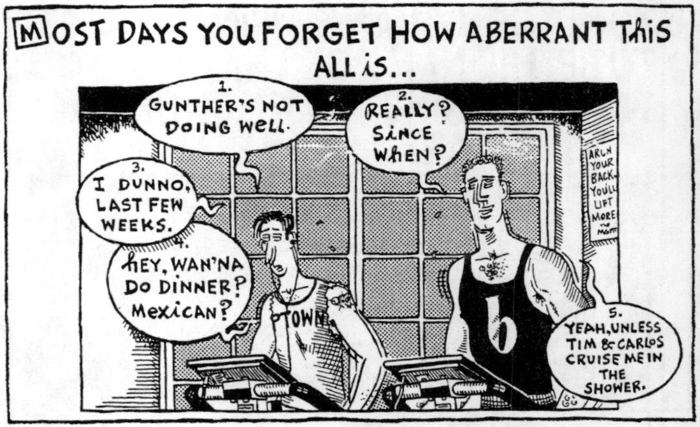
MOST DAYS YOU FORGET HOW ABERRANT THIS ALL IS...
1. GUNTHER'S NOT DOING WELL.
2. REALLY? SINCE WHEN?
3. I DUNNO, LAST FEW WEEKS.
4. HEY, WAN'NA DO DINNER? MEXICAN?
5. YEAH, UNLESS TIM & CARLOS CRUISE ME IN THE SHOWER.

OTHER TIMES THE WRONGNESS IS PLAIN. YOU DE-VOUR INFORMATION ABOUT DRUG COMBINATIONS, CLINICAL TRIALS, BABOON MARROW...

PEOPLE SEEM TO GET SICK IN WAVES.. THIS WEEK, THE TIDE'S IN..

Continued...

YOU RUN INTO AN OLD ACQUAINTANCE ON THE STREET AND REALIZE THAT YOU HAVE NOT LAID EYES ON HIM IN MONTHS. YOU'RE SWAMPED WITH RELIEF THAT HE DIDN'T DIE 8 OR 11 OR 16 MONTHS AGO, WHICH IS KIND OF SILLY GIVEN THAT A ½ HOUR BEFORE, YOU'D COMPLETLY FORGOTTEN HE EXISTED.

HEY ETHAN! LONG TIME NO SEE!

GUNTHER'S BEEN GOING TO A SUPPORT GROUP. HE CALLS IT "AIDS CLASS." ONE EXERCISE IS CALLED "UP AND OVER."

I RAISED MY HAND AND SUGGESTED IT BE CALLED "OVER & OUT" INSTEAD.

YOU'RE A DINK, GUNTHER.

end.

COPS, POPPERS & CRYiNG.

So YOU'RE DABBING ON A LITTLE "GENdARME", WHiCH, ACCORDING TO YOUR NEiGHBOR CHARLOTTE, MEANS "PARiSiAN TRAFFiC COP." THAT'S ONE DiFFERENCE BETWEEN YOU AND CHARL'; ƒHE ASSUMES A FRENCH COP WOULd SMELL BAd...

yuck.

WHAT? TOO STRONG? WHAT? TELL ME!

YOU'RE USiNG COLOGNE BECAUSE YOU'VE GOT A DATE WiTH JASON CHANG. WELL, NOT A DATE, EXACTLY, YOU OFFEREd HiM A RiDE TO GUNTHER'S MEMORiAL. YOU HOPE DOUG WON'T THiNK THAT'S TACKY OR WEiRD, ON THE OTHER HANd, DOUG HAD HiS CHANCE.

MONSiUER, did I JAYWALK? I'M AWFULLY SORRY! I GUESS iT'S TO THE BASTiLE FOR ME THEN, huh?...

Note: CARTOONIST All CAUGHT UP iN GALLiC FANTASY SORRY.

AND I SUPPOSE I'LL NEED A BiG STRONG, MUSTACHiOEd GUARD, YOU KNOW, TO PROTECT ME FROM THE JACOBiAN RABBLE.. CUZ THEY KNOW HOW CLOSE THE QUEEN AND I WERE BEFORE THEY, YOU KNOW, CHOPPED HER HEAD OFF... OH SURE, WE TALKED EVERY DAY.. I USEd TO DATE HER STYLiST, MiCHAEL, OH iT'S TRUE..

Continued...

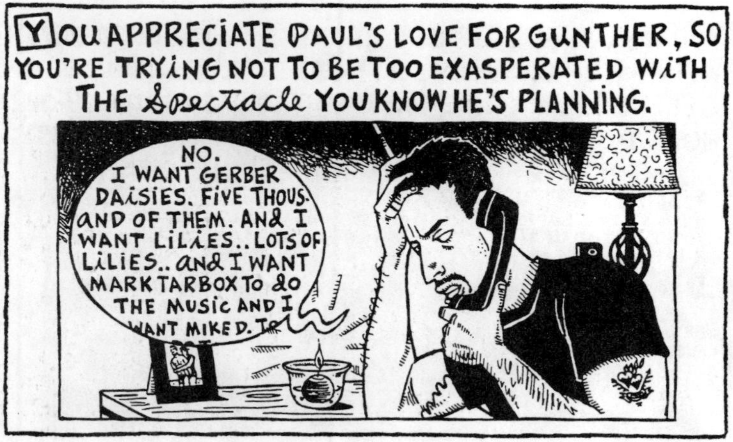
YOU APPRECIATE PAUL'S LOVE FOR GUNTHER, SO YOU'RE TRYING NOT TO BE TOO EXASPERATED WITH THE Spectacle YOU KNOW HE'S PLANNING.
NO. I WANT GERBER DAISIES. FIVE THOUSAND OF THEM. AND I WANT LILIES.. LOTS OF LILIES.. AND I WANT MARK TARBOX TO DO THE MUSIC AND I WANT MIKE D. TO

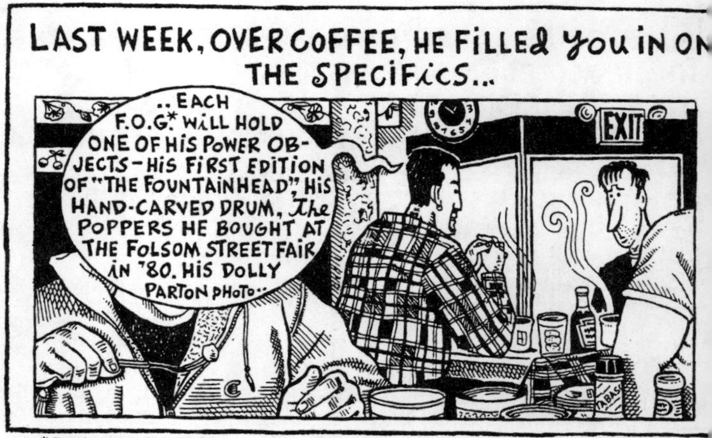
LAST WEEK, OVER COFFEE, HE FILLED YOU IN ON THE SPECIFICS...
..EACH F.O.G.* WILL HOLD ONE OF HIS POWER OBJECTS—HIS FIRST EDITION OF "THE FOUNTAINHEAD," HIS HAND-CARVED DRUM, THE POPPERS HE BOUGHT AT THE FOLSOM STREET FAIR IN '80. HIS DOLLY PARTON PHOTO...
EXIT
TABASCO

*FRIEND OF GUNTHER

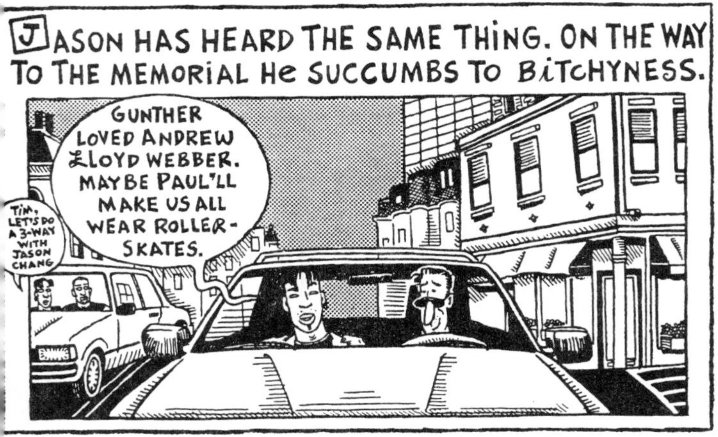
JASON HAS HEARD THE SAME THING. ON THE WAY TO THE MEMORIAL HE SUCCUMBS TO BITCHYNESS.
TIM, LET'S DO A 3-WAY WITH JASON CHANG
GUNTHER LOVED ANDREW LLOYD WEBBER. MAYBE PAUL'LL MAKE US ALL WEAR ROLLER-SKATES.

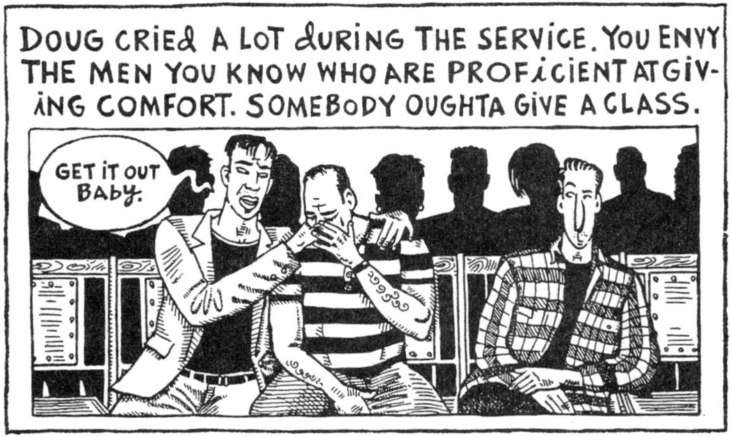
DOUG CRIED A LOT DURING THE SERVICE. YOU ENVY THE MEN YOU KNOW WHO ARE PROFICIENT AT GIVING COMFORT. SOMEBODY OUGHTA GIVE A CLASS.
GET IT OUT BABY.

end.

HOUSEGUEST FROM HADES...

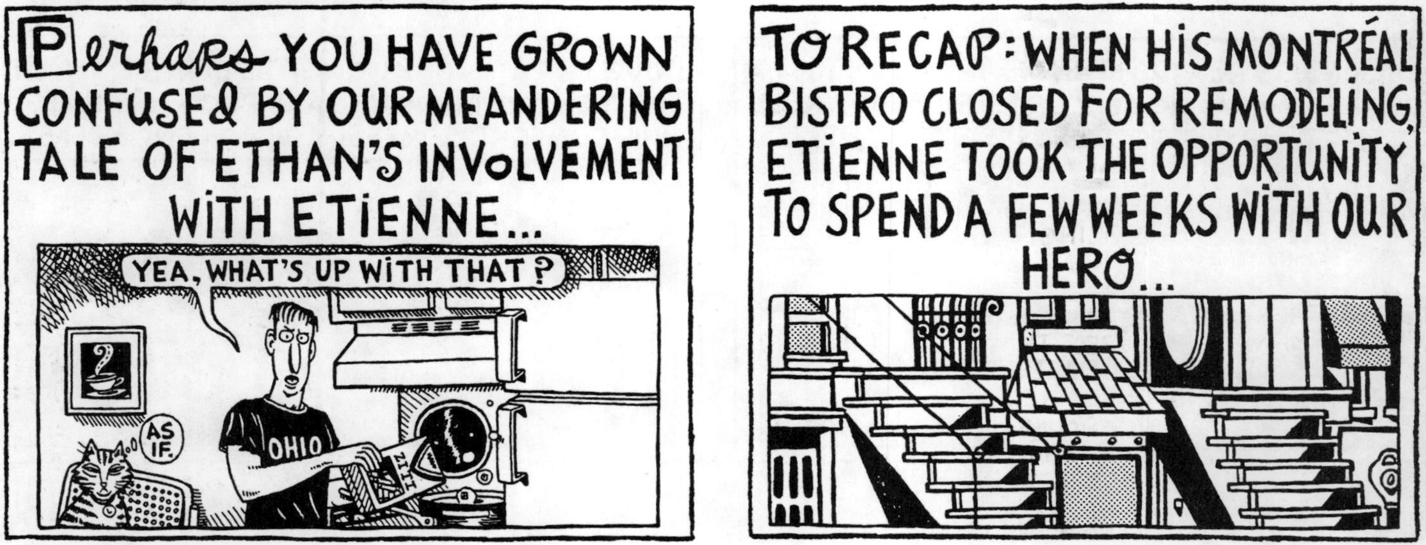

Perhaps YOU HAVE GROWN CONFUSED BY OUR MEANDERING TALE OF ETHAN'S INVOLVEMENT WITH ETIENNE...
YEA, WHAT'S UP WITH THAT?
AS IF.
OHIO
ZITI
TO RECAP: WHEN HIS MONTRÉAL BISTRO CLOSED FOR REMODELING, ETIENNE TOOK THE OPPORTUNITY TO SPEND A FEW WEEKS WITH OUR HERO...

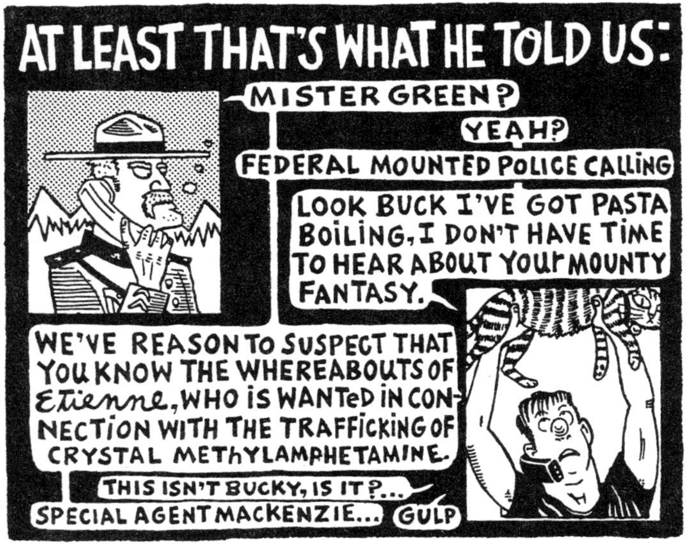
AT LEAST THAT'S WHAT HE TOLD US:
MISTER GREEN?
YEAH?
FEDERAL MOUNTED POLICE CALLING
LOOK BUCK I'VE GOT PASTA BOILING, I DON'T HAVE TIME TO HEAR ABOUT YOUR MOUNTY FANTASY.
WE'VE REASON TO SUSPECT THAT YOU KNOW THE WHEREABOUTS OF Etienne, WHO IS WANTED IN CONNECTION WITH THE TRAFFICKING OF CRYSTAL METHYLAMPHETAMINE.
THIS ISN'T BUCKY, IS IT?...
SPECIAL AGENT MACKENZIE...
GULP

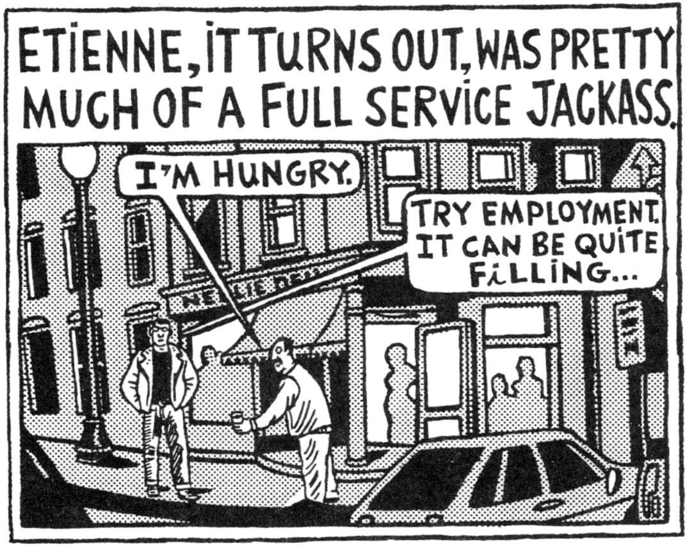
ETIENNE, IT TURNS OUT, WAS PRETTY MUCH OF A FULL SERVICE JACKASS.
I'M HUNGRY.
TRY EMPLOYMENT. IT CAN BE QUITE FILLING...

Continued...

HE WAS ALSO ONE OF THOSE PEOPLE WHO *hover* AT THE EDGE OF THE ROOM WHEN YOU ARE TRYING TO WATCH TV, WHILE NEVER ACTUALLY SITTING DOWN.

THAT'S NOT CATSUP, IT'S BLOOD.

IN CARTOON-TIME, ALL THIS MALEVOLENCE HAS BEEN GOING ON FOR QUITE A WHILE. IN THE TIME THAT YOU & I UNDERSTAND, ETIENNE'S BEEN ETHAN'S HOUSEGUEST FOR ABOUT 3½ DAYS.

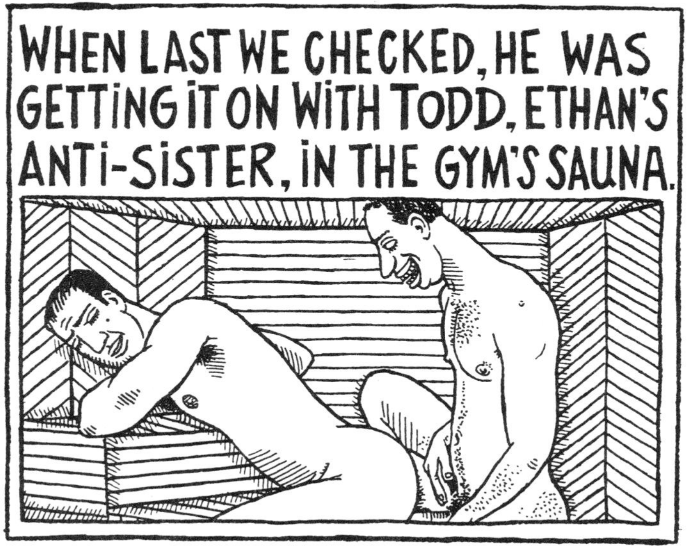
WHEN LAST WE CHECKED, HE WAS GETTING IT ON WITH TODD, ETHAN'S ANTI-SISTER, IN THE GYM'S SAUNA.

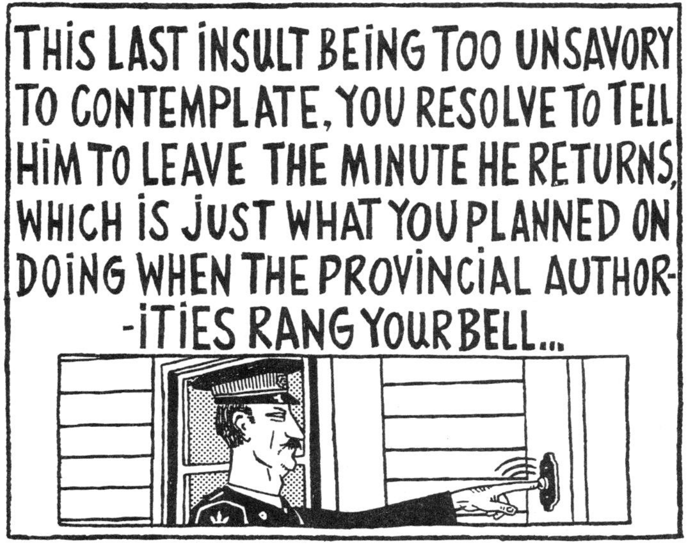
THIS LAST INSULT BEING TOO UNSAVORY TO CONTEMPLATE, YOU RESOLVE TO TELL HIM TO LEAVE THE MINUTE HE RETURNS, WHICH IS JUST WHAT YOU PLANNED ON DOING WHEN THE PROVINCIAL AUTHOR-ITIES RANG YOUR BELL...

END.

ANOTHER FESTIVE, DREADFUL, GET-TOGETHER.

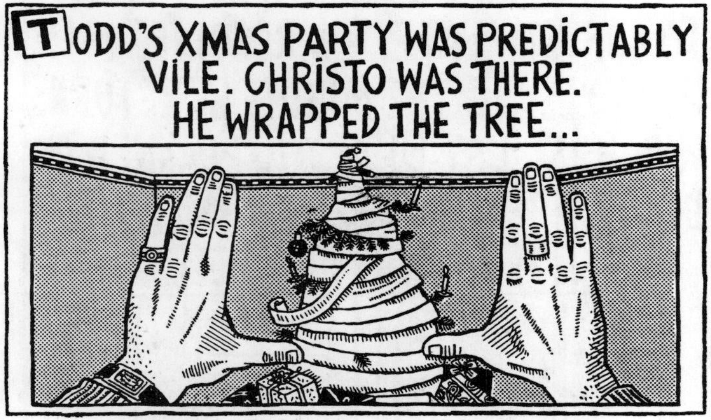
TODD'S XMAS PARTY WAS PREDICTABLY VILE. CHRISTO WAS THERE. HE WRAPPED THE TREE...

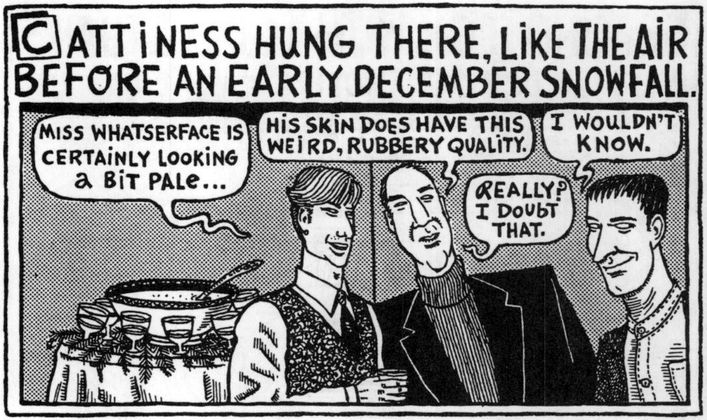
CATTINESS HUNG THERE, LIKE THE AIR BEFORE AN EARLY DECEMBER SNOWFALL.
MISS WHATSERFACE IS CERTAINLY LOOKING A BIT PALE...
HIS SKIN DOES HAVE THIS WEIRD, RUBBERY QUALITY.
I WOULDN'T KNOW.
REALLY? I DOUBT THAT.

YOU CONTRIBUTED A FABULOUS "LONDON BOY" WRIST WATCH TO THE HOLIDAY GRAB BAG. *alas*, YOUR SISTERS CAN BE A TACKY BUNCH. YOU WOUND UP WITH A LIME GREEN DILDO.

HEY! THE DECORATIVE CANDLES HAVE SET THE TREE'S WRAPPING ON FIRE... (SHRIEK) THE WHOLE THING'S ABLAZE...

OH JOY, ANOTHER DILDO.

OVER THE COURSE OF THE SEASON YOU'VE BORED & IRRITATED YOUR FAMILY OF FRIENDS WITH CEASELESS COMMENTARY ABOUT THE COMMERCIALIZATION OF CHRISTMAS.

YAMMER YAMMER YAMMER

SOMEBODY TURN THIS THING OFF... *JESUS*... AND BRING ME ANOTHER TANQUERAY.

Continued...

ANOTHER OF THE OPINIONS THAT YOU HARBOR, IS THAT MAYBE, JUST MAYBE, THE COMING YEAR WILL BE THE ONE IN WHICH, AT LONG LAST, YOU MEET THE MAN WHO YOU DECIDE TO SPEND YOUR LIFE WITH...
NOW YOU'RE TALKING! POWER OF POSITIVE THINKING! PICTURE HIM IN YOUR MIND. YOU CAN FIND HIM.. YOU WILL FIND HIM..
AT YOUR AGE? DREAM ON, MARY. ALL THE GOOD MEN ARE EITHER TAKEN, OR THEY'VE DATED EACH OF YOUR SEVENTEEN CLOSEST FRIENDS.

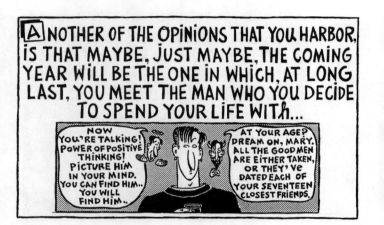

IN POINT OF FACT, NO ONE MUCH TAKES THESE OPINIONS OF YOURS TOO SERIOUSLY.
I KNOW YOU'RE DISAPPOINTED THAT FOR XMAS I DIDN'T GIVE A DONATION TO GMHC IN YOUR NAME, I JUST FELT LIKE BUYING YOU THESE BOOTS...
OH CHARL'
WOW
MAYBE I'LL SEND ETHAN GREEN A LOVER AND SOULMATE BEFORE THIS TIME NEXT YEAR.
.... ON SECOND THOUGHT, MAYBE I JUST BETTER WORRY ABOUT BOSNIA...

end.

NEW YEAR'S ...

YOU'VE BEEN ABANDONED BY ETIENNE. APPARENTLY FOR GOOD. HE LEFT A SUITCASE FULL OF EXPENSIVE SWEATERS. YOU'VE PUT THEM IN YOUR CELLAR...

(OK, OK, SO SOMEHOW THE DOLCE & GABBANA DIDN'T QUITE MAKE IT TO THE CELLAR.)

IT'S THE AFTERNOON OF NEW YEAR'S EVE. YOU'RE A LITTLE SURPRISED AT HAVING WASTED AN ENTIRE YEAR ON THIS GUY WHO YOU NEVER REALLY LIKED...

Continued...

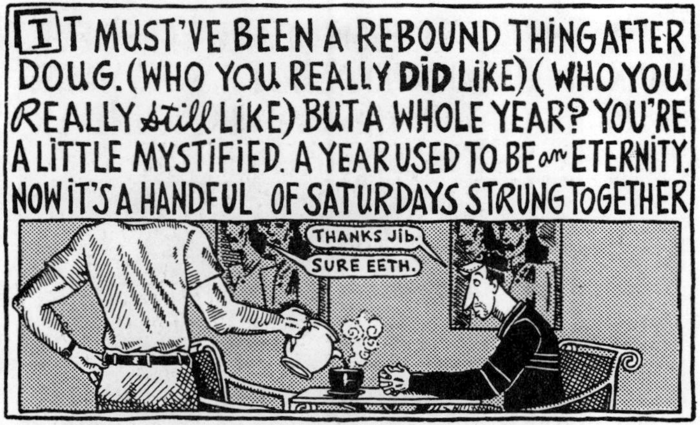
IT MUST'VE BEEN A REBOUND THING AFTER DOUG. (WHO YOU REALLY DID LIKE) (WHO YOU REALLY still LIKE) BUT A WHOLE YEAR? YOU'RE A LITTLE MYSTIFIED. A YEAR USED TO BE an ETERNITY. NOW IT'S A HANDFUL OF SATURDAYS STRUNG TOGETHER
THANKS Jib.
SURE EETH.

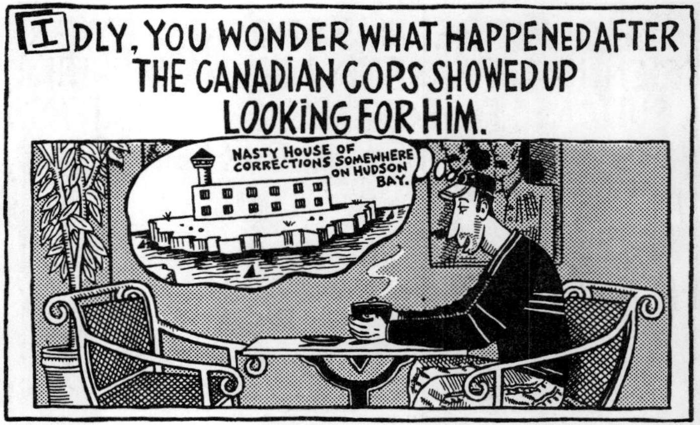
IDLY, YOU WONDER WHAT HAPPENED AFTER THE CANADIAN COPS SHOWED UP LOOKING FOR HIM.
NASTY HOUSE OF CORRECTIONS SOMEWHERE ON HUDSON BAY.

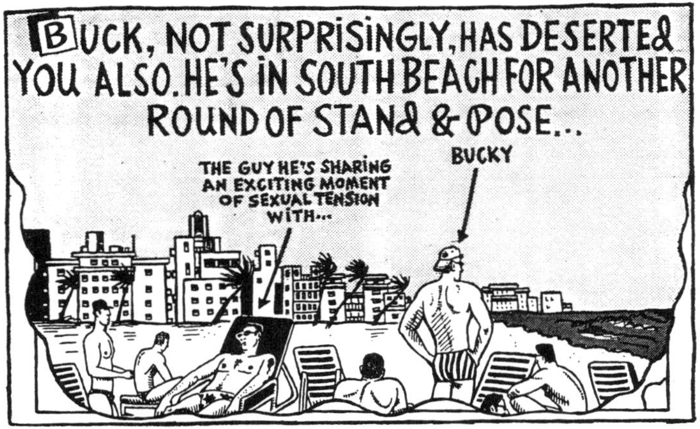
BUCK, NOT SURPRISINGLY, HAS DESERTED YOU ALSO. HE'S IN SOUTH BEACH FOR ANOTHER ROUND OF STAND & POSE...
THE GUY HE'S SHARING AN EXCITING MOMENT OF SEXUAL TENSION WITH...
BUCKY

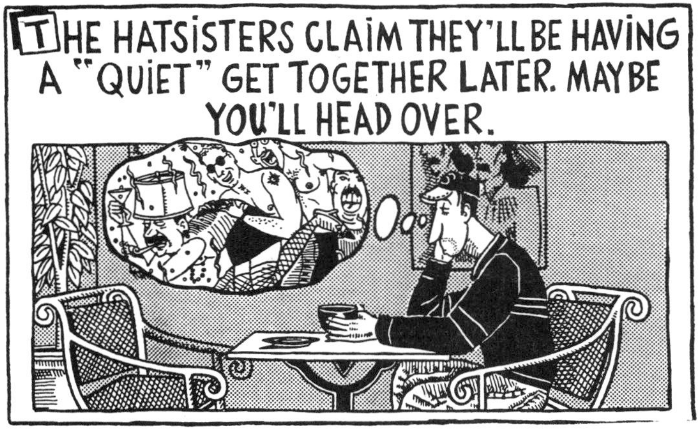
THE HATSISTERS CLAIM THEY'LL BE HAVING A "QUIET" GET TOGETHER LATER. MAYBE YOU'LL HEAD OVER.

end.

INFATUATION CONTINUED

IT'S BEEN MONTHS SINCE INFATUATION WITH JIM CONSUMED YOUR CONSCIOUSNESS LIKE BRUSHFIRE ON A MALIBU HILLSIDE...

AND LIKE ALL TRUE INFATUATIONS, THIS ONE WENT NOWHERE.
FAST.
giddyup.

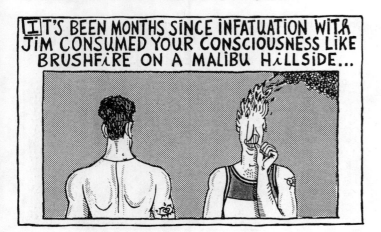

BUT YOU'VE LEARNED MORE RESILIENCY THAN YOU WOULD'VE THOUGHT, JUST A FEW YEARS AGO, YOU'D EVER BE CAPABLE OF.

C'MON, IZ THAT ALL Y'GOT? PLEAZE MARY, MY GRAMMA'S GOT MORE PUNCH..

SO WHEN IT BECAME CRYSTAL CLEAR THAT HE WANTED NOTHING TO DO WITH YOU, YOU STOPPED THINKING ABOUT HIM.

hi, UH, JIM, THIS IS ETHAN GREEN, WE MET AT THE BEACH, A FEW WEEKS AGO? I WAS WONDERING COUGH COUGH WOULD YOU LIKE TO GET A BITE TO EAT FOR SOMETHING, SOMETIME

ACTUALLY, I'M SEEING SOMEONE. HE'S SEXIER, RICHER, MORE SUC- CESSFUL, MORE ENGAGING, AND A BETTER DANCER THAN YOU, BUT, HEY, THANKS FOR ASKING..

I'VE GOT ANOTHER CALL CIAO

Continued...

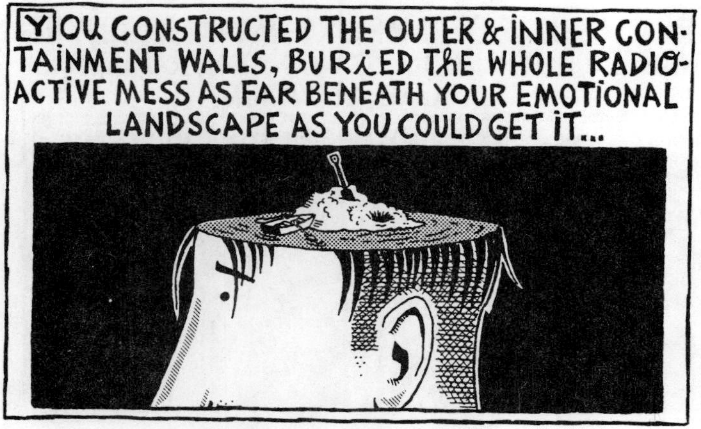
YOU CONSTRUCTED THE OUTER & INNER CONTAINMENT WALLS, BURIED THE WHOLE RADIOACTIVE MESS AS FAR BENEATH YOUR EMOTIONAL LANDSCAPE AS YOU COULD GET IT...

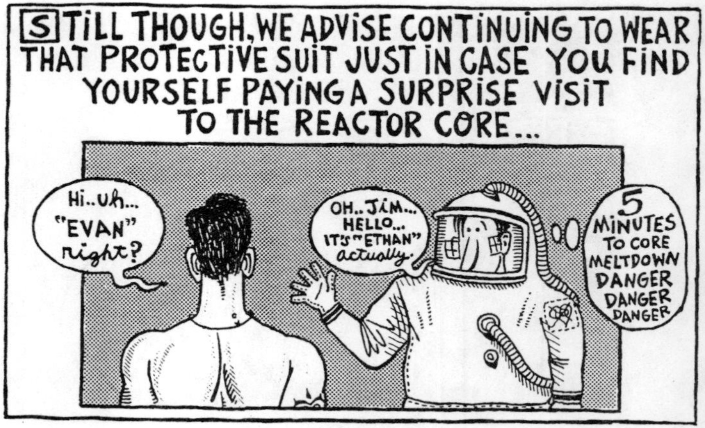
STILL THOUGH, WE ADVISE CONTINUING TO WEAR THAT PROTECTIVE SUIT JUST IN CASE YOU FIND YOURSELF PAYING A SURPRISE VISIT TO THE REACTOR CORE...
Hi.. uh... "EVAN" right?
OH.. JIM... HELLO... IT'S "ETHAN" actually.
5 MINUTES TO CORE MELTDOWN DANGER DANGER DANGER

THE
end.

By Eric ORner

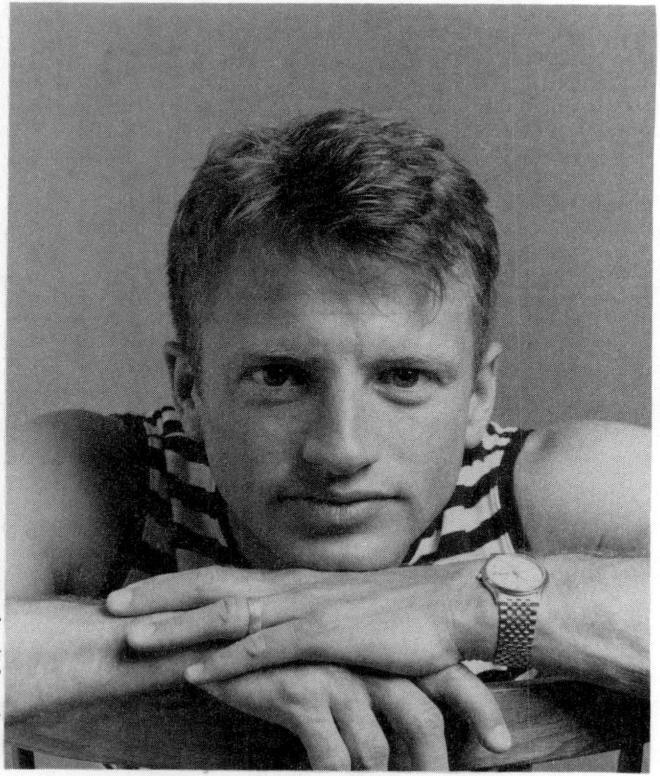

Author photograph by Stella Johnson

About the Author

Eric Orner lives and works in Cambridge, Massachusetts. He has been writing and drawing "The Mostly Unfabulous Social Life of Ethan Green" since 1989. "Ethan" appears in about sixty alternative newspapers in the United States, Canada, and Great Britain, and has been collected into two previous books published St. Martin's Press: *The Mostly Unfabulous Social Life of Ethan Green* (1992) and *The Seven Deadly Sins of Love* (1994).